ASPECTS OF GREEK AND ROMAN LIFE

General Editor: H. H. Scullard

* * *

THE NOBLEST ROMAN

M. L. Clarke

THE NOBLEST ROMAN

Marcus Brutus and His Reputation

M. L. Clarke

CORNELL UNIVERSITY PRESS
Ithaca, New York

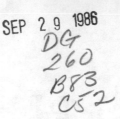
First published 1981

International Standard Book Number
0–8014–1393–1
Library of Congress Catalog Card Number
80–69178

Printed and bound
in the United States of America

CONTENTS

PREFACE

On the Ides of March in the year 44 B C Julius Caesar was stabbed to death by a group of Roman nobles led by Marcus Brutus. The victim, Caesar, has an obvious appeal to posterity; he if anyone was a great man in the conventional sense. Yet Brutus, the 'noblest Roman of them all', the man of principle who killed his benefactor and whose action proved disastrous to himself and to Rome, is in some ways a more interesting character. Shakespeare at any rate thought so when he made him the dramatic hero of a play nominally about Julius Caesar.

Shakespeare's Brutus is sensitive and scrupulous, an idealist who fails partly because of his very virtues. Others have seen him in a different light. Dante put him with Judas Iscariot in the lowest circle of Inferno. In the eighteenth century he was looked up to as the heroic champion of freedom and was admired as a model of ancient virtue, to be classed with Cato, and even with Socrates. In *Gulliver's Travels*, when Brutus is called up from the dead, Gulliver sees in his countenance 'the most consummate Virtue, the greatest Intrepidity, and Firmness of Mind, the truest Love of his Country, and general Benevolence for Mankind'. Yet this was the man who was almost universally depreciated in the nineteenth century. His critics could not forgive his extortionate money-lending in Cyprus; they condemned him as weak, obstinate, self-righteous.

When a man has been so variously judged it is unlikely that any assessment can claim finality. I have however done my best to give a reliable account of him based on the ancient evidence, and this occupies the first half of the book. The second deals with his reputation in after times, how he has been regarded by historians and political philosophers, poets and dramatists. For like other major figures from antiquity Brutus has had a posthumous life, and this is part of history no less than the life which ended at Philippi in 42 B C.

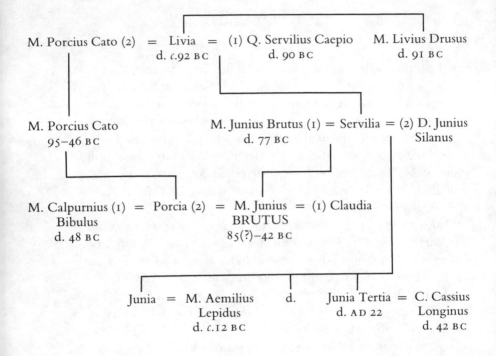

M. Porcius Cato (2) = Livia = (1) Q. Servilius Caepio   M. Livius Drusus
                      d. c.92 BC   d. 90 BC   d. 91 BC

M. Porcius Cato   M. Junius Brutus (1) = Servilia = (2) D. Junius
95–46 BC   d. 77 BC   Silanus

M. Calpurnius (1) = Porcia (2) = M. Junius = (1) Claudia
Bibulus   BRUTUS
d. 48 BC   85(?)–42 BC

Junia = M. Aemilius   d.   Junia Tertia = C. Cassius
        Lepidus   d. AD 22   Longinus
        d. c.12 BC   d. 42 BC

CHAPTER ONE

BRUTUS IN HISTORY

I THE COMING MAN

We begin with the family, always an important thing for a Roman of the upper class and particularly important for Brutus. Marcus Junius Brutus, to give him his full name, came of a famous line. He claimed to be descended from the founder of the Roman Republic, the Lucius Junius Brutus who, according to tradition, expelled the last of the kings, Tarquinius Superbus, in 509 BC, served as the first consul of the new republic and in that capacity passed sentence of death on his sons for their part in a plot to restore Tarquinius. Other members of the family had held the consulship in later ages. In the second century there was a Brutus who was an eminent jurist, and another, his son, was notorious for constantly appearing in the courts as a prosecutor. Brutus's father was a victim of the aftermath of the civil war between Marius and Sulla. An adherent of the Marian party, he held the tribunate in 83; he later joined the unsuccessful revolt of Lepidus and was in command at Mutina, where he surrendered to Pompey and was put to death in cold blood in spite of Pompey's promise to spare him. His wife Servilia, Brutus's mother, was the daughter of Q. Servilius Caepio and Livia, sister of M. Drusus the reforming tribune of 91 BC. Divorced from her first husband Caepio, Livia married M. Porcius Cato and by him became mother of the famous Cato, Cato Uticensis, who was thus Brutus's uncle. After the elder Brutus's death Servilia married Decimus Junius Silanus, consul in 62, and by him had three daughters. Two of these married men who were to play an important part in history; one was wife of Lepidus the triumvir, another of Cassius, Brutus's associate in the conspiracy against Caesar. Thus when Brutus and Cassius in Shakespeare's *Julius*

Caesar address one another as brother it is more than a metaphor; Brutus was half-brother of Cassius's wife.

With this family background it was only natural that Brutus should look to a political career and expect to play a leading role in public life. He was one of the *nobiles*, the 'well-known people', to give the original sense of the Latin word. The Roman nobility was not a close caste. A noble family was one whose members in the past had held the highest offices of state; its present representatives would naturally aim at following in the footsteps of their ancestors, but in theory they had no advantages over those who could not claim nobility, and all alike could hold office only through election by the citizen body. Family sentiment was not, as it once was in modern Europe, bound up with inherited titles, armorial bearings and feudal privileges. It was at its worst an arrogant assumption that the prizes of political life were reserved to the descendants of those who had previously held them and an unscrupulous use of wealth and power to ensure their continued enjoyment; at its best, and we may count Brutus among the best of the Roman nobility, it was a creditable desire to emulate one's ancestors by serving the state at home and on the field of battle.

The family however meant something more than this for Brutus. Emulating his ancestors meant a particular political attitude, one of opposition to any form of despotism. There was his descent from Lucius Brutus, whether real or imaginary (the sceptical could point out that as his sons had been put to death he could have left no descendants of his name); and on his mother's side he could claim a champion of freedom as ancestor, the Servilius Ahala who had killed Spurius Maelius in the fifth century on the ground that he was a potential tyrant, an act which won him a place in the political mythology of Rome as a hero of republicanism. These family traditions undoubtedly had a strong influence on Brutus. When he served as one of the *tresviri monetales*, the officials in charge of the Roman mint, probably in 54 BC, one of the coins he issued bore a head of Libertas with a representation of Lucius Brutus on the reverse, while another had L. Brutus's head on one side and that of Ahala on the other.[1] In his house were portrait busts of the original Brutus and of Ahala which, as Cicero observed, he could see every day. He also had a family tree in which the two ancestors figured, drawn up at his own request by Atticus, who though older than Brutus numbered him as well as Cicero among his close friends.[2]

Brutus was probably born in 85 BC. According to Cicero his birth was ten years after Hortensius's first appearance as an advocate, which, again according to Cicero, was in 95 BC. Velleius Paterculus however states that he was in his thirty-seventh year at his death in 42.[3] We thus have two dates for his birth, 85 and 79 or 78, and the statement in the epitome of Livy that he died aged about forty is compatible with both. If, as is generally accepted, Brutus was quaestor in 53, he must have been at least thirty by that year, and even if other evidence tends on the whole to support the date given by Velleius, the authority of Cicero, a contemporary and friend of Brutus, has more weight than that of a historian writing more than seventy years later.[4]

Brutus's mother Servilia was a woman of character, ambitious and energetic, at home in the male world of Roman politics. She was indeed on terms of intimacy with Julius Caesar. She is described as being madly in love with him, while for Caesar himself this was, according to Suetonius, the most serious of his numerous love affairs.[5] It was said that Caesar was actually the father of Brutus, and though the story is not taken seriously by scholars, it has had a certain appeal to literary men in the past (witness its use by Voltaire and Alfieri) and cannot therefore be entirely ignored. Its source is Plutarch, according to whom Caesar himself was inclined to believe that Brutus was his son; and Caesar's alleged remark when he saw Brutus among his assassins 'You too, my child?' (καὶ σὺ τέκνον;) points in the same direction, though Suetonius, who records these last words, does not specifically refer to the supposed relationship.[6] In fact it is far from plausible. Plutarch has a story about a note from Servilia sent to Caesar during a Senate meeting in 63 BC; Suetonius mentions a costly present given by him to her during his consulship of 59, and a clear hint in a letter of Cicero of that year shows that the two were, or were believed to be, lovers at that time.[7] The affair evidently belonged to a period long after Brutus's birth. As for Caesar's alleged last words, Suetonius also records, and evidently prefers, another tradition according to which after a groan when first struck he said nothing at all.[8]

Having lost his father at an early age Brutus was drawn into his mother's family. He was indeed adopted by one of them, and from M. Junius Brutus became officially Q. Caepio Brutus, though his adoptive name was seldom used. The Caepio who adopted him is generally taken to be a brother of Servilia, but his identity is not known for certain. He may have died soon after the adoption, and in any case it is likely that the influence on Brutus of his new father was small in comparison to that of his mother and of his uncle Cato. Whether under Cato's influence or not, he had a thorough education in grammar and rhetoric, Greek and Latin, and in philosophy, which could only be studied in Greek. His teacher in grammar, a term which included literature as well as language, was Staberius Eros, who like many of the early teachers at Rome was an ex-slave. He is said to have taught free of charge the sons of those proscribed by Sulla, and it may therefore be that his political affiliations commended him to Brutus's family. Appropriately enough, Brutus's future associate Cassius was also one of his pupils.[9]

Though the name Eros suggests a Greek origin Staberius was a Latin grammarian and Brutus probably went to a different teacher for his Greek lessons. Whoever this was, he acquired a knowledge of the classics of Greek literature, particularly Homer and the dramatists, which will have meant more to him than the rather clumsy early Latin epic and drama which he would have to study in the Latin grammar school. He continued his bilingual education in the next stage, that of rhetoric. He was well trained in Latin rhetoric, but by whom is not recorded.[10] Greek rhetoric he may well have begun at Rome, but he continued its study in the Greek world when, like other young Romans at that time, he went abroad to complete his education. At Athens he was taught by Pammenes, described by Cicero as by far the most eloquent man in Greece, under whom he made a special study of Demosthenes, and in Rhodes, then a noted centre for rhetorical study, his teacher was Empylus, who became a member of his household and after his death wrote a memoir of him. Another Greek rhetorician who became a friend of his was Strato, who was with him at his death and, according to one account, held the sword on which he fell.[11]

At Athens there was more to be learnt than the art of speech. The city was the headquarters of philosophy, the home of the three schools, Academic, Peripatetic, Epicurean and Stoic. Brutus heard what each had to say and gave his allegiance to the Academy. The head of the Academy at that time was Aristus, a man with an attractive personality though of no great intellectual distinction; Brutus studied under him, and was sufficiently impressed by him to have him for a time as a member of his household.[12] The American jurist Max Radin, who wrote a book about Brutus, after stating correctly that he declined to adhere to Stoicism or Epicureanism, went on to say: 'Even the Academics of his day, who professed a critical scepticism about all philosophical pronouncements, were too dogmatic for him. He preferred to keep examining propositions rather than to assert them.'[13] This is very wide of the mark. Neither Brutus nor the Academics of his day were sceptical and undogmatic. This was the position of the 'New Academy' of Carneades and his followers which had by now given place to a less negative version of Academic doctrine. Antiochus of Ascalon, who was head of the school in the 70s, claimed to be reviving the original teachings of the school, with the confusing result that the 'new' Academy was followed by what claimed to be the 'old' Academy. After his death the headship of the school passed to his brother, Brutus's teacher Aristus, whose views appear to have been indistinguishable from those of Antiochus.

Antiochus maintained that the Stoics had taken their philosophy from the Academy and had merely invented a new terminology, and Academic doctrine as interpreted by him was close to that of the Stoics. With a few changes, said Cicero, he would have been a complete Stoic.[14] The difference was that, according to Stoic doctrine, virtue alone was sufficient for a blessed, or happy, life and bodily goods were of no account, whereas Antiochus held that such goods contributed something, though very little; virtue by itself was sufficient for the blessed life but not for a life supremely blessed. Cicero himself was never quite happy about this and argued against both Antiochus and Aristus on the point. He could not see how one could be truly happy when suffering from bodily ills if these really were ills; the Stoic view, which denied that they were ills and made virtue the only good, was more logical than that of Antiochus.[15] Not that Cicero ever committed himself to Stoicism; he remained an Academic, though critical of Antiochus's innovations. Brutus too remained loyal to the Academy, in spite of the influence of his uncle Cato, who was a committed Stoic.[16]

Brutus was no mere dilettante student. Like Cato he took his philosophy seriously and made it his guide to life. At the same time there was a more genial atmosphere about the Academy, even under Antiochus and Aristus, than about Stoicism. It was not harsh and narrow as Stoicism could be. It was associated with statesmanship and oratory, humane studies and the graces of style. Brutus shared in the hellenized culture of the Roman nobility of his day. Quotations from Greek poetry came readily to his lips, and he lived in style and elegance. At one of his country houses there was a stream to which he gave the name of Eurotas, the river on which Sparta stood, and a Persian Colonnade named after a building in that city; another of his villas was, it seems, not Sparta but Athens, with a room called Parthenon.[17] He was something of a collector. He had a bronze bust of Demosthenes; and his admiration for a statuette of a boy by Strongylion was such that it came to be known as 'Brutus's boy'.[18] He was interested in history, and used to engage in the seemingly tedious and uncreative work of epitomizing existing historical works.[19] He also wrote verse, though without much success; according to Tacitus his poems were no better than those of Cicero but he was more fortunate in that fewer people knew of them.[20] His activities as a poet suggest that there was a lighter side to what was essentially a serious, even solemn character, and in this connection mention should perhaps be made of the story found in a late and not very reliable source that he was among the lovers of the actress Cytheris, the mistress of Mark Antony and the Lycoris of Gallus's love poems.[21] All one can say is that this seems unlikely. Brutus had learnt from philosophy self-control and distrust of the emotions. He was very different from the flamboyant Antony, who to Cicero's disgust was openly going about with Cytheris in 49 BC. One would expect his attitude to have been similar to that of Cicero, who, after finding himself to his embarrassment in Cytheris's company at a dinner party, wrote to a friend: 'I was never much interested in that sort of thing even when I was young, much less now in my old age.'[22]

How long Brutus pursued his studies in Greece we do not know. He was certainly in Rome in 59, when he makes his first appearance on the political scene in connection with the affair of Vettius and his alleged plot to murder Pompey. When the plot came to Pompey's ears and the senate ordered an investigation Vettius implicated a number of Roman aristocrats including Brutus. Owing, it was believed, to the intervention of Servilia with Caesar, he soon withdrew Brutus's name, and in any case he was a man of dubious character whose allegations were probably groundless.[23] This was the year of Caesar's first consulship and his alliance with Pompey and Crassus, cemented in the former case by Pompey's marriage with his daughter Julia. Julia had previously been betrothed to another man whom our sources name as Caepio or Servilius Caepio.[24] Was this, as has been suggested,[25] none other than Brutus? Surely not. According to Suetonius this Caepio had given Caesar valuable assistance against Bibulus, which hardly fits Brutus, nephew of Bibulus's father-in-law Cato. And if the ousted suitor was Brutus he would surely have been recorded under the name by which he was known to posterity. We must dismiss the intriguing idea of Brutus as prospective son-in-law to his mother's lover and his future victim.

The alliance of Caesar, Pompey and Crassus was indirectly responsible for Brutus's first important assignment. The triumvirs wanted their leading senatorial opponents, Cicero and Cato, out of the way. Whereas Cicero was exiled, Cato was treated with more consideration. He was given the task of organizing the annexation of Cyprus, which Rome had decided to take over from the Egyptian dynasty by which it was then ruled. He left Rome in 58, taking Brutus with him. There was no resistance to the Roman annexation. The island's king Ptolemy committed suicide, and Brutus was given the task of taking charge of his property. He had gone to Pamphylia to recuperate after an illness, but was summoned from there, took on the job, though reluctantly, and completed it successfully, taking to Rome the money which had been realized. Like Cato, he could be trusted to be honest in his handling of public money. At the same time, as we shall see later, he was quite ready to engage on his own account in a lucrative financial arrangement with the authorities of Salamis, the chief city of Cyprus.

In 54 (if this date is correct) Brutus was, as has already been mentioned, one of the three moneyers, or mint masters, in Rome. This was a post normally held by young men of good family at the outset of their political career. Their names appeared on the coins they issued, and it was common for the designs to have some reference to the moneyer's family. In the case of Brutus there must have been some political significance in his choice of Lucius Brutus and Ahala, not to mention Libertas personified, and his coins can perhaps be related to the rumours of a dictatorship for Pompey which Cicero records in letters of 54 and his laments about the end of the old free republic.[26] In any case they marked him out as one who could be expected to champion freedom and oppose autocracy. But in order to display these qualities to good effect and to acquire a position of influence in politics he must make his way up through the various stages of the *cursus honorum*, beginning with the quaestorship. This he held in the next year, 53, serving in the province of Cilicia, which now included the island of Cyprus. The governor under whom he served was Appius Claudius, whose daughter he had married in the previous year. By this marriage he became connected with an old and famous Roman family, but a family some of whose present members were hardly worthy of their ancestry. Brutus's wife had as uncle Cicero's great enemy the demagogic tribune Publius Clodius and as aunt the disreputable Clodia of whose goings-on Cicero gives a vivid picture in his *Pro Caelio*. Appius himself, who unlike his brother and sister retained the patrician spelling of the family name, was more conventional and respectable. He was something of a mixture. He was an unscrupulous politician, and Cicero, who succeeded him as governor of Cilicia, was appalled at the way he had treated the province. None the less he evidently had likeable qualities; Cicero was anxious for his friendship, and found him a pleasant companion who shared his scholarly interests.[27]

Appius Claudius returned to Rome in 51, to face trial for misconduct in his province and for bribery in his campaign for election as censor. As was only right in view of their relationship, Brutus spoke in his defence, and the combination of his advocacy and that of the elderly and eminent Hortensius secured acquittal. Brutus, who had returned to Rome a year before his father-in-law, was making a name for himself as an advocate and pleaded a number of other cases about this time.[28] Particulars of these have not been recorded, but we know something of a speech he wrote as a rhetorical exercise and not for delivery, a defence of Milo, who was put on trial in 52 for killing P. Clodius. Cicero, who appeared as advocate for Milo at the trial, based his case on the argument that Clodius had lain in wait for Milo and that the latter had in effect killed him in self-defence. Brutus's line was to claim that Clodius was justly killed as an enemy of the state.[29] Milo did not deny his responsibility for the death of Clodius, and his defence presented an advocate with the challenge of making the best of a very weak case. But it cannot have been only this that made Brutus try his hand. By declaring Clodius a bad citizen justly killed he was aligning himself with Cicero and the senatorial party against Caesar and the popular party. More significant perhaps was the fact that he was ready to argue in favour of assassination on grounds of state.

It was in this year that the disturbed state of Rome led to the appointment of Pompey as sole consul to restore order. He did not abuse his unprecedented position, but to Brutus the situation was too much like a despotism. He was as much opposed to autocracy when exercised by Pompey as he later was when Caesar was the enemy of freedom, and he attacked Pompey in a speech the circumstances of which are unknown. 'It is better,' he said in the course of it, 'to have no one under one's command than to be the slave of another; in the former case it is possible to live honourably, in the latter life is no life.' But the speech was not all on this high level. It also included a personal attack on Pompey, who was accused of having his hands steeped in the blood of his fellow citizens, an allusion presumably to his early career and in particular to the killing of Brutus's father.[30] Brutus had a somewhat tenuous family connection with Pompey in that a sister-in-law of his, one of Appius Claudius's daughters, was married to Pompey's eldest son, but this had done nothing to bring him closer to one whom he would naturally regard as an enemy.

Brutus was a coming man, whose talents and character, added to his family connections, made him, as Cicero said to Appius Claudius after the latter's acquittal, 'first among the younger generation and soon, I hope, to be first man in the state'.[31] Cicero had got to know him before he left Rome to succeed Claudius as governor of Cilicia. At the instigation of Atticus he had given him every encouragement, and he was beginning to be fond of him.[32] When Cicero reached Cilicia he found Brutus's friendship something of an embarrassment. Two Roman business men, Scaptius and Matinius, were strongly recommended to him by Brutus, and one of them, Scaptius, came to see him to enlist his support in exacting a sum of money owed to them by the city of Salamis in Cyprus.[33] Scaptius had had the support of Appius Claudius, who had conferred on him the rank of prefect, which gave him the prestige of official recognition though without specific functions. Claudius had also provided him with a troop of cavalry to intimidate the Salaminians, and this had acted to such effect that five of the city councillors, besieged in their Council House, had been starved to death. Cicero, who had been met by a deputation from Cyprus even before he reached the province, ordered the cavalry to withdraw, and, when Scaptius asked him to renew his appointment as prefect, he refused, on the ground that he never gave such a rank to business men. He promised however to see that the Salaminians paid what they owed.

The situation proved to be somewhat complex. Six years earlier the Salaminians had wanted to raise a loan in Rome, but had found that a recently passed law forbade loans to provincial communities by Roman citizens in Rome. Scaptius however had agreed to make a loan, at 48 per cent, if this was safeguarded by a senatorial decree, and through Brutus's influence a decree was passed indemnifying the parties concerned, while another decree laid down that the governor of Cilicia should 'give judgment according to the bond'. A further complication was that the Senate had later passed a decree fixing 12 per cent as the legal rate of interest, and Cicero, in the edict he issued on taking up his governorship, stated that he would observe this rate. He did not feel that he could go against this undertaking in the case of the Salaminians, to say nothing of his unwillingness to see the community ruined by the higher rate of interest. He brought the Salaminians to the point of agreeing to pay the whole debt at 12 per cent compound interest, an offer which was, however, refused by Scaptius.

The next development was that Cicero discovered to his surprise that he had been misled by Brutus. The loan had been made not by Scaptius and Matinius, as he had been led to believe, but by Brutus himself, and the other two were merely his agents. Cicero was not at all pleased with Brutus. If, he wrote to Atticus, Brutus thought he ought to have insisted on 48 per cent, if he was going to complain of Cicero's refusal to confer a prefecture on Scaptius or of his recalling the troop of horse, 'I shall be sorry to have incurred his displeasure but far sorrier to find that he is not the man I took him for'. Brutus was saying nice things about Cicero in letters to Atticus, but to Cicero he adopted 'a brusque arrogant ungracious tone'.[34]

Brutus's financial interests were not confined to Salamis. He had also lent money to Ariobarzanes, whose kingdom of Cappadocia was adjacent to Cilicia, and he enlisted Cicero's help in exacting the interest. This case did not present the same difficulties as that of the Salaminians. Cicero did his best to secure payment, though he believed the king was completely bankrupt, and he was quite willing to confer prefectures on two Romans who were looking after Brutus's interests in Cappadocia, since they were not carrying on business in his province.[35]

Brutus has been severely criticized by modern writers for his money-lending activities, and with some justice. This is not simply a matter of applying modern standards to the ancient world; extortionate money-lending was in accord neither with the traditional moral code of the Roman aristocracy to which Brutus belonged nor with the teaching of Greek philosophy which he professed to follow. It is true that Atticus, a humane and cultivated man, saw nothing wrong with it, or, if he did, considered that friendship should prevail over strict morality; no doubt it is also true that other contemporary Romans did worse things in the provinces. But Brutus, who wrote one book on Virtue and another on Duties, might expect to be judged by the highest standards. The best that can be said for him is that the Salaminians had voluntarily agreed to a loan on certain terms (and the rate of interest would not seem so outrageously high), and it was only right that these terms should be observed. It may be, too, that he was unaware of some of the things done by his agents.[36] He may well have thought of himself as a benefactor of the Salaminians; he was not the sort of man to think himself anything but in the right. As for Cicero, he seems to have soon forgotten the incident. His irritation with

Brutus was short-lived, and he continued to regard him with esteem and affection.

After his return from Cilicia Brutus, as we have seen, was beginning to become known as an advocate, and in normal times he would have proceeded to stand for the higher offices of state. His career was, however, cut short by the civil war between Caesar and Pompey. That he should join Pompey, as he did, was by no means a foregone conclusion. Hitherto he had had no personal dealings with the man responsible for his father's death, and a few years previously he had openly attacked him. But political principle came before personal feelings, and he now decided that Pompey's cause was that of the republic. He was not with Pompey when he left Italy and withdrew across the Adriatic in the face of Caesar's march on Rome. He accepted the post of legate to Sestius, a staunch supporter of Cicero, who was now proconsul of Cilicia. Soon however he left the province to join Pompey. He was an asset to the cause morally if not militarily, and Pompey, so it was said, was so delighted at his arrival that he rose from his seat and embraced him as a superior in the sight of all. Caesar too would have been glad to have him on his side, and is said to have given orders to his officers to make sure that he was not killed in battle.[37]

According to Lucan, Brutus was at first in favour of holding aloof from the war and joined Pompey only as a result of Cato's advice and example. This, however, inspired him to what Lucan calls an excessive desire for civil war, excessive perhaps by contrast with Cato's rational calculations of the good effect his own adherence would have on Pompey.[38] We can well believe that Brutus had grave doubts about Pompey as a champion of constitutionalism, but when once he had made up his mind he certainly appears to have been a wholehearted adherent, for writing from Pompey's camp in June 48 Cicero reported to Atticus that he was zealous in the cause.[39] This could hardly have been said of Cicero himself, who had joined Pompey after much hesitation and with no enthusiasm and when he reached the camp only made himself unpopular by his sneers and criticisms, and who stayed behind sick at Dyrrhachium when Pompey followed Caesar eastwards to meet him at the disastrous battle of Pharsalus. Unlike Cicero, Brutus took an active part in the fighting, though he had the ability to abstract himself from his surroundings, and before the battle, after an exhausting march in the summer heat, while others were asleep or had their minds on the approaching engagement, occupied himself with making an epitome of the Greek historian Polybius.

After Pompey's defeat at Pharsalus Brutus quickly made his peace with Caesar, was pardoned by him and warmly welcomed. Pompey had fled after the battle, and according to Plutarch Caesar took Brutus for a walk and asked him what he thought was Pompey's destination; Brutus indicated, rightly, that he was making for Egypt, as a result of which Caesar at once hurried there.[40] It would not be to Brutus's credit if he really helped Caesar to pursue the man under whom he had so recently served; but there are good reasons for doubting Plutarch's story. More credence should be given to Caesar's account, according to which it was only when he reached Asia Minor and learnt that Pompey had been seen in Cyprus that he guessed he was making for Egypt.[41]

Pharsalus did not mean the end of the civil war. It was not until nearly three years later that the last Pompeian forces were defeated. Caesar arrived in Egypt to find that Pompey had been murdered as soon as he set foot on shore. In Alexandria, Caesar nearly came to grief through overconfidence, but eventually extricated himself, settled the kingdom to his satisfaction, and was able to leave in the spring of 45. Before he returned to Rome affairs in the east demanded his attention. Among those involved was Deiotarus, king of Galatia, an old ally of Rome who had supported Pompey, but had changed sides after Pharsalus and had rendered some services to Caesar's cause. While confirming his title of king, Caesar made him give up some of his territory to neighbouring potentates who also had some claim on him. The case was heard at Nicaea and Brutus, who had remained in the east since Pharsalus, spoke on behalf of the king. Whether his advocacy had any influence is not clear, but at any rate Caesar was impressed by the force and freedom with which he spoke.[42]

On his way back to Italy Brutus visited M. Marcellus, a supporter of Pompey who had retired to Mytilene after Pharsalus, and was much impressed by his bearing. He also stopped at Samos, where he found another leading Roman, the highly respected jurist Servius Sulpicius, and had some instruction from him in

Roman pontifical law.[43] When he was once more in Rome there was no doubt how he stood with Caesar, for he was appointed proconsul of Cisalpine Gaul for the year 46, in spite of having held no office higher than quaestor. It was from this province, a peculiar one, geographically part of Italy and thoroughly Romanized, that Caesar had crossed the boundary line, the river Rubicon, to march on Rome, and it was a sign of his confidence in Brutus that he appointed him to this key position. Brutus proved a model governor. According to Plutarch his proconsulship meant relief and consolation to the people after their previous misfortunes, and it was commemorated by a statue of him in Milan.[44]

While he was, by Caesar's favour, holding this honourable post, Caesar was engaged in fighting against the Republican forces in North Africa. Among their leaders was Cato, and it may be asked why Brutus was not to be found at his uncle's side. Cato was not present at Pharsalus to give advice and strengthen resolution; Brutus had to make his decision on his own. In doing so he may well have reasoned as Cicero did. Cicero had come to the conclusion that a decision should be determined by the outcome of the battle of Pharsalus. He had expected that after his victory Caesar would soon be back in Rome and the Republic, though impaired, would none the less survive; as it was, the delay caused by Caesar's preoccupations in the east meant the revival of Pompeian hopes and the prolongation of civil war.[45] According to Cicero Cassius, who had also assisted Pompey and then made his peace with Caesar, shared these views; it is likely enough that Brutus, who had been seeing Cicero in Pompey's camp, had come to the same conclusions. They would be reinforced by personal considerations; he had never been in rapport with Pompey, and Caesar was ready to extend to him a flattering attention. Whatever his reasons, he made his decision and having done so was prepared to make the best of public life under Caesar. Disillusion was to come soon.

2 THE INTELLECTUAL

The years 46 and 45 were marked by a close association between Brutus and Cicero based on their common intellectual interests, and on Cicero's side by a number of literary works addressed to, or named after, Brutus. It began with a letter sent by Brutus to Cicero from Asia Minor, a letter, as Cicero puts it, of 'wise advice and friendly encouragement'. Brutus showed a tact which was sometimes lacking in his dealings with Cicero, and included some references to his past services of the sort that were meat and drink to him. He was naturally pleased to be told that his deeds would speak of him, silent though he was, that they would outlive him and bear witness to his political wisdom whatever the fate of the Republic. The letter aroused Cicero from his state of depression and despondency. It was, he said, like the first Roman victories after the disaster of Cannae which encouraged the Romans to look forward to further successes; in the same way 'after the grievous disasters which both I and Rome as a whole have suffered nothing happened to me until Brutus's letter that was in accordance with my wishes or could in some degree alleviate my worries'.[1] At the same time Atticus wrote for Cicero a chronological summary of history the receipt of which added to the effect of Brutus's letter and encouraged him to return to intellectual pursuits. It also helped him in the composition of the first of his literary works of this period, his history of Roman oratory in the form of a dialogue between himself, Brutus and Atticus, to which he gave the title *Brutus*.

Now that his voice had been silenced it was not unnatural that he should reflect on the art which he had practised with such success and look back on its earlier history. It was natural too that he should associate Brutus with such a work, for Brutus was himself an orator of note. His reputation in this respect slumped after his death. Quintilian considered his philosophical work superior to his oratory, and one of the speakers in Tacitus's Dialogue on Orators says much the same, adding that even his admirers admitted that he hardly deserved his reputation as an orator. Both Quintilian and Tacitus, however, acknowledge his *gravitas*, his weight and dignity.[2] Cicero, as we shall see later, had rather different views from his on oratorical style; but he felt naturally drawn to a young man who like himself combined oratory with philosophy and had learnt his philosophy from the Academy.

In ordinary times Brutus might have succeeded to the position which Cicero had held in the forum; as it was, there seemed little prospect of his being able to display his talents. Eloquence was silenced just at the time when Cicero would willingly have given place to him.³ Yet he was not completely without hope. Towards the end of *Brutus* there is a passage which deserves to be quoted in full:

When I consider your case, Brutus, I am filled with sorrow. You were a young man racing ahead to the applause of all when across the path as it were of your chariot came the misfortunes of our country. This is the sorrow which afflicts me, this the concern which worries me, as it does Atticus here, who shares in my affection and esteem for you. You have our goodwill, we want you to enjoy the fruits of your virtue, we pray for a political situation in which you can renew and enhance the memory of the two distinguished families from which you are sprung. The forum was yours, the field was open to you; you were the one person who had brought to it not only a tongue sharpened by rhetorical training but also an eloquence enriched by a profound culture which enabled you to unite the honour conferred by virtue with the high renown which eloquence brings. Our concern regarding you is twofold; your absence from politics is both a loss to Rome and a loss to you. None the less, Brutus, though this disaster to the commonwealth has so inopportunely hampered your progress, maintain your studies uninterrupted and ensure for yourself what you have already nearly, or I should rather say completely ensured, that you stand out from the crowd of advocates whom I have assembled in this conversation of ours.⁴

Too much has sometimes been read into this passage. 'With perfidious skill,' wrote Boissier, Cicero 'interested his vanity in the restoration of the ancient government by pointing out what a position he might make for himself in it . . . Antony was not altogether wrong when he accused Cicero of having been an accomplice in the death of Caesar.' A more recent writer, J. P. V. D. Balsdon, goes further. The *Brutus*, he writes, 'concluded with the suggestion that Caesar should be killed and that Brutus should kill him . . . How, except by murder, could Brutus do as well as or even better than those ancestors of his?'⁵ These interpretations are surely misconceived. The modern scholar knows what happened on the Ides of March, and reads words written some two years earlier in the light of that knowledge. Cicero and his readers had no foreknowledge of the future. Moreover, there is no mention here of

Lucius Brutus or Ahala; when Cicero prays for a situation in which Brutus can live up to the traditions of his family he does not of course mean one which demands tyrannicide, but one in which Brutus can play a normal part in public life. At the time of writing there was no saying how things would turn out, and it was natural enough that Cicero should entertain some hopes of a restoration of the free republic. He certainly had such hopes when he wrote the *Brutus* and after. It was in September of 46 that Caesar's pardon of Marcellus led him to think he saw some signs of the republic coming to life again and to express his hopes in a speech of thanks to Caesar in the Senate.[6]

At one point in the dialogue Cicero makes Brutus say that he does not mind missing the rewards of oratory because what he really enjoys is the study and practice of speaking.[7] We cannot of course take the *Brutus* as a record of an actual conversation, but it had more actuality than most of Cicero's dialogues, and this particular remark is in character. For Brutus was a keen student, and he shared Cicero's interest in the theory of rhetoric. He had his own ideas on style. He criticized the rhythm of a passage in Demosthenes which everyone else found perfectly satisfactory; he did not share Cicero's admiration for Isocrates; he deliberately avoided smoothness of style and as a result often fell into iambic rhythms.[8] Cicero thought his oratory slack and disjointed, while Brutus in turn criticized that of Cicero as, to give a literal translation of his words, 'broken' and 'with a disjointed hip', which seems at first sight much the same as what Cicero said of Brutus. It is not easy to catch the nuance of these stylistic metaphors, but remembering that *fractus* (broken) can convey the idea of effeminacy and that Quintilian records with indignant surprise that Cicero was criticized as not sufficiently masculine in his rhythms, we can get some idea of what Brutus had in mind.[9]

His criticisms seem rather disrespectful in view of Cicero's age and eminence as an orator, but they were made in a friendly spirit and were not resented. The letters in which they were expressed are no longer extant, but we have the treatise *Orator* addressed to Brutus in which Cicero expounded his views on the best type of oratory with special reference to rhythm. This was written in response to a request from Brutus and, it would seem, with some reluctance. One might be inclined to dismiss as a literary convention the rather frequent references to pressure from Brutus, but they are confirmed by a letter to Atticus where Cicero speaks of the work being undertaken 'as a result, one might almost say, of Brutus's own entreaties'. Perhaps he knew that there was no chance of his converting Brutus to his views. And in fact he did not.[10]

Behind the *Orator* lie not only Cicero's discussions and correspondence with Brutus but also the criticisms of another younger orator Calvus, who had died in 47, the year before its publication. Calvus was the leader of the 'Atticists', who rejected as 'Asiatic' what they considered the bombastic over-rhythmical redundant style of Cicero and cultivated a straightforward simplicity like that of the Athenian Lysias. Brutus has sometimes been counted as one of the Atticists. Indeed one classical scholar carelessly attributed to Plutarch the statement that his oratory was Attic, an error which was reproduced in a standard English commentary on Shakespeare's *Julius Caesar*. What Plutarch says is that in Greek Brutus cultivated a laconic brevity, a remark based on some of Brutus's Greek letters and of no relevance to his Latin oratory.[11] He may have been one of Cicero's critics, but there seems to be no good ground for counting him among the Atticists.[12] Cicero certainly does not associate him with them. In the *Brutus* he makes Brutus refer to Calvus's ambition to be an Attic orator without any suggestion that he shares this ambition, and in works dedicated to Brutus he speaks disparagingly of the Atticists as he would hardly have done if Brutus had been one of them.[13] If he had any leanings in that direction Cicero's aim was to discourage them and by assuming that he had no truck with the Atticists to detach him from the movement.

The *Orator* is a more personal document than might at first appear. Apart from the number of times Brutus is addressed by name, which remind us that he is not simply the recipient of a formal dedication, there are some references to him which have little relation to his views on oratorical style. At the beginning of the work Cicero refers to their affectionate feelings for one another, and later on he writes:

It is a great and arduous task that I am undertaking, Brutus, but love knows of no difficulties. And love is what I feel and have always felt for your abilities, your learning and your character. And I am fired daily more and more not only by the longing which overwhelms me as I miss our companionship and familiar intercourse and your scholarly conversation, but also by the remarkable reputation that your admirable qualities have won you, those qualities which though apparently incompatible are united by wisdom. Could there be any two things so different as strictness and affability, yet was anyone ever more upright or more genial than you? What is harder than to settle numerous disputes and still retain universal popularity? Yet you succeed in sending away satisfied and contented even those against whom you give an adverse decision; and the result is that though you do nothing by way of favour you find all you do favourably received.[14]

Inevitably one contrasts these passages with the not always complimentary references to Brutus in Cicero's letters to Atticus. Writing for Brutus and with a view to publication he perhaps exaggerated the good qualities of his friend and the warmth of his feelings towards him. The suspicion arises too that there was an element of policy in this; Brutus, who was then governor of Cisalpine Gaul, stood well with Caesar, and Cicero wanted to make it clear that he stood well with Brutus. In one respect such suspicions are supported by contemporary evidence. In February 46, after the defeat of the Republicans in North Africa, Cato put an end to his life. At Brutus's suggestion Cicero wrote a eulogy of him, and he slips into the *Orator*, shortly after the passage we have quoted, a reminder that Brutus shared the responsibility for this publication.[15] One contemporary at least, a friend of Cicero's who was in exile and doubtful about his prospects of returning, took this as designed to safeguard Cicero's position with Caesar.[16] But what may be true of the almost parenthetical reference to Cicero's *Cato* does not necessarily apply to all that he says of Brutus. It is possible to be too sceptical, as it is to be too credulous, about Cicero's sincerity. He may have written with a warmth which he did not always feel, but there is no doubting that Brutus had qualities which could arouse affection as well as admiration.

The suicide of Cato, unbending to the last in his opposition to despotism and supported by his philosophy, made a strong impression on the ancient world and caused him to be canonized as a kind of saint of Stoicism. At the time, however, his admirers had

some doubts about his action. Both Brutus and Cicero adhered to
the Academy, and Plato, the founder of the school, had held it
wrong to take one's own life. Though Brutus was eventually to
follow his uncle's example, at first he disapproved of his action,
thinking it impious and unmanly. As for Cicero, in an earlier work
he had accepted Plato's view, but now he modified it; he allowed
that we are forbidden by God to leave this life except at his bidding,
but maintained that there were none the less occasions when God
offered good reasons for doing so, as he did to Cato, and then the
wise man would joyfully exchange the darkness of this world for
the light of another. But there was still a difficulty. If it was right
for Cato to take his life, should not the other Republicans who did
not follow his example have done so instead of surrendering to
Caesar? He answered this question by suggesting rather tentatively
that nature had given men different characters and that what was
appropriate for one of Cato's character might not be for others.[18]
These uncertainties and hesitations may well reflect not only
Cicero's thoughts but also those of Brutus.

Cicero's eulogy of Cato was followed by one from Brutus's pen.
This appears to have been an ineffective production. Cicero was
very critical of one part of it, that which concerned the punishment
of the Catilinarian conspirators in 63 BC. This was the year of
Cicero's consulship when, as he never forgot and would not let
others forget, he saved the state. Cato had also played some part in
those events. When the Senate debated the fate of the conspirators
he had made a powerful speech in favour of the death penalty, and
Brutus naturally included a reference to this. But according to
Cicero he got his facts wrong in his account of the debate, and he
failed to give Cicero himself sufficient credit for his part in sup-
pressing the conspiracy; his reference to him as an 'excellent consul'
was altogether too faint praise.[19] Caesar's reaction to the two
eulogies was highly gratifying to Cicero. He professed to judge
them solely on style, and was far more complimentary to Cicero
than to Brutus. His own style, he claimed, had been improved by
his repeated readings of Cicero's work, whereas after reading that
of Brutus he felt himself by comparison a good writer.[20] Caesar
knew how to flatter. Brutus did not.

In February 45 Cicero's beloved daughter Tullia died and Brutus dutifully wrote to console him. The letter was sensible and friendly but brought him no consolation.[21] When the time came for Brutus himself to be consoled, for the death of his second wife, Cicero recalled this letter.

I would perform the same duty as you did in my grief and would console you by letter but for my knowledge that in your sorrow you have no need for those remedies by which you alleviated mine. I hope you may find it easier to heal yourself than you did to heal me. It would be out of keeping with the elevation of your character to be unable yourself to do what you bid others do. For my part I was deterred from excessive grief both by the arguments you adduced and by your authority; for since you thought I bore my loss with less fortitude than became a man, especially one accustomed to console others, you used stronger words of rebuke in your letter than was your wont. And so, setting great store by your judgment and respecting it, I pulled myself together and accounted all that I had learnt read and heard of more weight because supported by your authority.[22]

It would seem from this that Brutus wrote in rather severe terms. This was no doubt his style, and Cicero did not resent it. Though the letter did little to console him he felt, as he said to Atticus, that if Brutus had been there in person he could have been of some help 'because he is so fond of me'.[23]

Later that year Brutus had his own personal preoccupations. He decided to divorce his wife. What reasons he had for getting rid of Claudia we do not know. Cicero wrote to Atticus in June to say that the divorce was not generally approved, but what the grounds were for this disapproval is not clear. Brutus no doubt intended to remarry, but if he had already decided on his future wife when he arranged the divorce Cicero, who was evidently not in his confidence on this matter, was unaware of his decision.[24] It was not long, however, before marriage took place, and his new wife was his cousin Porcia, daughter of Cato and widow of Bibulus. For those who look for political motives in Roman marriages this alliance presents a problem. All Porcia's family associations were anti-Caesarian and the marriage can have brought Brutus no political advantage at a time when Caesar was all-powerful. It looks more like a deliberate move to show opposition to Caesar, until one reflects that at that time Brutus was still in high favour with

Caesar and still apparently thinking well of him. Perhaps after all, if the phrase is not too sentimental, it was a love match. At any rate, whatever influence Porcia may have had later, it can hardly be taken as marking a turning point in Brutus's political attitude.

Porcia had had three sons by her previous marriage and of these the only surviving one was old enough to go to Athens to study in 45 BC, to be a candidate for the augurate in 43, and to fight with Brutus at Philippi.[25] She cannot therefore have been in her first youth when she married Brutus.[26] She was well suited to him, and proved a loyal and loving wife.[27] There were, however, some difficulties at first. She did not get on well with Servilia. In July 45 Cicero told Atticus that the two ladies were being inconsiderate in quarrelling with one another when Brutus was behaving dutifully to both of them.[28] Servilia may have been a possessive mother, but she should by now have got used to having a daughter-in-law, and it may be that there was more in these quarrels than ordinary jealousy. An imaginative biographer can read a good deal into them, remembering that Servilia, though half-sister to Cato, Porcia's father, had been mistress of Caesar, and assuming that her wish was to draw her son closer to her old lover. 'For two years,' writes Max Radin, 'these two women engaged in nothing else than a bitter struggle for the soul of Brutus.'[29] It may be so. But it is well to remember that this is based on a single sentence in a letter of Cicero and that his comment is simply: 'Very tiresome, but that's what life is like.'

Personal troubles and preoccupations put some strain on the relations between Brutus and Cicero during the summer of 45. We do not know what was behind the displeasure that Cicero felt early in May at Brutus's failure to visit him when he was at his villa at Cumae, but it was presumably his grief at the loss of Tullia which some weeks later made him reluctant to accept Brutus's hospitality at Tusculum, where both of them had villas.[30] Then in July he confides to Atticus that at the moment his state of mind and that of Brutus are such that they cannot live in one another's society.[31] An uninhibited social intercourse seemed impossible while each of the two had other things to think about (it was about this time that Brutus's marriage took place). There was no alienation between the two men and the sensitive Cicero may have felt these inhibitions more than Brutus did. We get the impression, however, that they were not quite so close to one another as Cicero would have liked. Atticus, though a little older than Cicero, seems to have found it easier to be on intimate terms with Brutus than Cicero did; it is interesting to see that Cicero has to go to him when he wants to be assured about Brutus's affection for him.[32]

Intellectually the two men were still closely associated. Cicero was engaged on that series of philosophical works which he produced with great rapidity after Tullia's death, and of these works three, *De Finibus*, the *Tusculan Disputations* and *De Natura Deorum*, were dedicated to Brutus.[33] He was a fitting recipient, for he had a strong interest in philosophy; he had encouraged Cicero in his philosophical writing, and had dedicated to him his own philosophical treatise, *De Virtute*.[34]

Brutus had learnt from Aristus that virtue was sufficient to ensure a happy life. It followed from this that the good man was independent of fortune; faced with poverty, ill health or exile he could, as Horace put it, wrap himself up in his own virtue. This self-sufficient virtue Brutus expounded in what was evidently, to judge by the little we know of it, no dry and abstract treatise. He observed that it was sufficient consolation to the exile that he could take his virtue with him. He recalled seeing Marcellus in exile in Mitylene and, so far as his nature allowed, living a perfectly happy life; Brutus claimed that the prospect of returning to Rome without Marcellus made him feel that it was he who would be an exile rather than the man he was leaving, and maintained that Caesar had refrained from stopping at Mitylene because he could not bear to see Marcellus. The reader was left with an impression of sincerity; 'You can tell he means what he says,' was Quintilian's comment.[35]

In addition to *De Virtute* Brutus wrote a treatise *De Patientia*, of which we know virtually nothing, and a work on Duties, *De Officiis*, or rather, for Brutus apparently used a Greek title, περὶ καθήκοντος [36] Cicero also wrote a *De Officiis*, based on a Greek work περὶ τοῦ καθήκοντος, and one wonders what was the relation between the two. Cicero's was not completed until towards the end of 44 B C, when Brutus had already left Italy, and one would therefore expect it to have been preceded by that of Brutus. But Cicero makes no mention of Brutus's work either in his treatise or in his

correspondence, and it may be that in spite of the identity of title
the two works were on different lines. We know that Brutus had
much to say on duties within the family, those of parents, children
and brothers, subjects which Cicero left alone.[37]

In the works dedicated to him Brutus would have read with
particular interest the final book of De Finibus, in which Cicero
expounds the views of Antiochus, which Brutus shared, and the
last book of the Tusculan Disputations, where he argues that virtue
by itself is sufficient for a happy life, a dogma, as Cicero says,
particularly dear to Brutus and expounded by him in many conversations with Cicero as well as in his De Virtute.[38] In both books
Cicero makes some criticisms of Antiochus, but they are not
pressed home very vigorously and in Tusculans V he prefers to
stress the points of agreement between different schools rather than
to argue disputed points. He introduces the book with a moving
passage which Brutus can hardly have read with indifference. After
referring to the blows of fortune which he had suffered and which
at times shook his faith in the sufficiency of virtue for the blessed
life he pulls himself up:

Here I blame myself for judging the strength of virtue by the
weakness of others and perhaps of myself too, not by virtue itself.
If there is such a thing as virtue – and your uncle, Brutus, has
removed any doubts one might have on that score – it rises superior
to all the accidents that may affect a man, despises them, spurns the
mishaps of mankind, and free from all blame counts everything
irrelevant but its own self; whereas in our case fear magnifies all
misfortunes in advance and sorrow magnifies them when upon us,
and we put the blame on the nature of things rather than on our
error. But for this fault and all other vices and wrongdoings on our
part the remedy lies with philosophy. O philosophy, guide of life,
you who discover the way to virtue and banish vice, what should
we have been, and not only we but the very life of man, without
you? . . . I fly to you, seek help from you, and to you commit
myself, as I did to a large extent before now but now do wholly and
entirely. For one day led well and in accordance with your precepts
is to be preferred before an immortality of vice.[39]

Brutus may not have shared the almost religious exaltation to
which Cicero here gives expression. But he had a faith, perhaps
steadier and less fitful than Cicero's, in philosophy and in the self-

sufficient virtue which it preached. He was to need that faith to sustain him in what was to come.

3 THE CONSPIRATOR

After his victory over the republican forces in Africa in 46 Caesar returned to Rome and put through some reforming measures, but in November he was forced to leave again, this time for Spain to deal with the forces under Pompey's sons which were still in control there. His victory at Munda in March of the next year left him indisputably master of the Roman world. Brutus, who had no official position after his return from Cisalpine Gaul, continued to hope that he would return to constitutionalism. In July he was encouraging Cicero in a project, which came to nothing, of writing a letter of advice to Caesar, and a little later, when Caesar was on his way back from Spain, he himself went to meet him, and came back with the impression that he was moving towards constitutionalism. Cicero disapproved of his expedition, and hearing of the favourable impression he had received thought he was deserting the traditions of his family.[1] He may have thought this even more when Brutus was appointed *praetor urbanus* for the year 44, for Caesar now controlled all such appointments and his choice of Brutus strengthened the latter's obligation to him. At the same time Cassius was made *praetor peregrinus*, so that these two former enemies of Caesar, pardoned by him and now enjoying his favour, held the two senior praetorships at the time when they conspired against him. Brutus was specially favoured. Caesar preferred him to Cassius for the post of *praetor urbanus* in spite of the latter's seniority and military distinction.[2]

Gaius Cassius Longinus, who was to be inseparably associated with Brutus for the rest of his life, had won a reputation as a skilful and energetic soldier and administrator when he served with Crassus on his disastrous expedition against the Parthians. After the Roman defeat at Carrhae he escaped to Syria, reorganized what was left of the Roman army and successfully defended the province against Parthian attacks. He held the tribunate in 49, joined Pompey in the civil war, and was given a naval command by him. After Pharsalus he made his peace with Caesar, and even served under him as *legatus* in the campaign against Pharnaces,[3] after which he returned to Italy where he was living in 46 and 45. He was a hot-tempered man with a sharp tongue and not without wit. Like Brutus he had philosophical interests, but unlike Brutus he adhered to the school of Epicurus. There are some letters of Cicero to him written in humorous vein rallying him on his Epicureanism, which he had recently adopted in place of Stoicism.[4] This conversion Cicero called deserting virtue seduced by the allurements of pleasure, in reply to which Cassius claimed that pleasure depended on virtue and that the Epicurean 'lovers of pleasure' were really lovers of goodness and justice.[5] In one respect, however, Cassius conspicuously failed to follow Epicurus. The Epicurean ideal was a quiet and undisturbed life, free from the worries of politics. The best course was, as Lucretius put it, 'to obey in peace'.[6] This is just what Cassius was not prepared to do. It is true that at the beginning of 45, comparing Caesar with Pompey's son, he told Cicero that he preferred the lenient master he knew to a cruel and untried one.[7] But his subsequent career showed that he was not prepared to submit to any master. It was said in antiquity that by contrast with Brutus he disliked the ruler rather than the rule, that he was an enemy of Caesar rather than of tyranny, and that he was led to conspire against him by certain personal grievances. Plutarch, however, who records this view of his motives, does not accept it, and maintains that Cassius had always been hostile to tyranny whoever exercised it, and Cicero says much the same of the family into which he was born.[8]

The conspiracy to kill Caesar, though more than sixty persons were involved, was a well kept secret and we cannot therefore expect to know with any accuracy what went on as the plot developed. Our best contemporary source, Cicero's letters, fails us, for Cicero was not privy to the conspiracy and in any case his letters are scanty for the crucial period. When men began to think seriously of assassination we do not know. After Caesar's return from Spain in September 45 his behaviour was increasingly arbitrary, and any hopes that might still be entertained of a return to constitutional government must soon have faded. Then in February of the next year came what must have been for some at least the decisive event, Caesar's appointment as dictator for life. This, says

Plutarch, was clear tyranny.⁹ The dictatorship was traditionally a temporary expedient, an appointment for a limited period in time of crisis. Even Sulla, a despot as powerful as Caesar and less beneficent, had given up the dictatorship and retired to private life. Caesar now made it clear that he intended to keep hold of power.

There was not only the reality of power; there were also the outward marks, those honours which Suetonius lists: a statue among those of the kings, a special seat in the form of a raised couch at the theatre, a golden throne in the Senate House and on the tribunal, a chariot and litter for his statue to be carried with those of the gods at the procession in the Circus, temples, altars, statues, a cushioned seat like those on which effigies of the gods were displayed, new religious cults associated with him, a month given the new name of July in his honour.¹⁰ Then there was the insolence of his underlings and his own indifference to the susceptibilities of the senators; finally there was the impression he gave that in spite of all denials he wished, and even intended, to take the title of king. All this was intolerable to men who had some pride and self-respect and feeling for the traditions of Roman public life.

It is sometimes said that Brutus, the doctrinaire intellectual, derived his ideas about the virtue of tyrannicide from Greece, and Greek sentiment certainly may have had some influence on him. 'The Greeks', said Cicero, 'give divine honours to those who have killed tyrants. Think of what I have seen in Athens and other Greek states – the cults instituted in honour of such men, the hymns, the songs; they are worshipped and commemorated almost like immortals.'¹¹ Brutus also knew the Greek world. He had seen the statues of Harmodius and Aristogeiton in Athens; he may have declaimed against tyranny in the Greek schools of rhetoric. On the other hand there was little to encourage a love of liberty, or political activism, in the philosophies of the day, and the fact that other Romans less intellectual and less steeped in Greek culture were involved in the plot suggests that Roman traditions were at least as powerful an influence as Greek. Anti-monarchical sentiment was in fact strong at Rome. The Romans had not forgotten that they had once been ruled by kings but had freed themselves from such rule. Lucius Brutus had his statue in Rome as Harmodius and Aristogeiton had theirs in Athens. He had not actually killed

Tarquinius, though his statue showed him with drawn sword, but there was plenty of precedent for assassination in the history of the Republic, and it was all too easy to justify it as the killing of a potential tyrant. Perhaps we should say that Greek and Roman ideas had merged in Brutus's thought as they had in Cicero's. In his *De Republica*, which was published seven years before the death of Caesar and which one would expect Brutus to have read, Cicero adopted the Greek distinction between king and tyrant, the good and the bad type of monarch; he attempted to apply the Greek theory of constitutional cycles to Roman history, and gave Tarquinius Superbus as an example of a king who degenerated into a tyrant. He depicted the tyrant as a creature so loathsome as to be no longer human, and promised more on that theme when he came to those who had aimed at despotic power after the establishment of the Republic. The manuscript breaks off soon after this promise, but it is virtually certain that in addition to some names from early Roman history he gave Tiberius Gracchus as an example of a would-be tyrant.[12] If the murder of Gracchus could be defended as tyrannicide it was not difficult to justify that of Caesar.

None the less Brutus might well have hesitated before he committed himself to killing a man to whom he was so much indebted. Caesar was Brutus's friend at least in the sense that he had shown him marked favour, but whether there was that degree of affection between the two that some modern writers have postulated is doubtful. A young man might well have mixed feelings about his mother's former lover, and there seems to be no firm evidence that Caesar for his part had any very warm feelings towards his former mistress's son. He used to say of him, 'It's a great question what he wants, but whatever it is he wants he really does want it.' (magni refert hic quid velit, sed quicquid vult valde vult).[13] The remark hardly suggests a relationship of sympathy and understanding. Indeed there are grounds for thinking that Caesar found Brutus positively unsympathetic; according to our sources he joined him with Cassius as one of those with 'a lean and hungry look' whom he preferred not to have about him.[14]

Even if there was no bond of affection between the two men, obligation and mutual services nevertheless played a large part in ancient ideas of friendship, and Brutus, author of a book on duties, would have been very conscious of what he owed to Caesar. It was only after pressure from Cassius that he joined in the conspiracy. This at any rate is Plutarch's account, followed by Appian, and it seems more plausible than that of Dio, who makes Brutus take the lead from the beginning.[15] According to Plutarch the friends whom Cassius first sounded thought that Brutus's reputation was such that it was essential for him to be brought in. 'The undertaking demanded not violence or daring but the reputation of a man like him who would as it were consecrate the victim for sacrifice and guarantee the justice of the act by his mere presence. Without him they would be less confident in action and more open to suspicion after it. Brutus, it would be said, would not have refused to take part if the deed was an honourable one.'[16] Cassius therefore approached Brutus. He asked if he intended to be present at the Senate meeting due to take place on 1 March when, so he had heard, a move was to be made to have Caesar declared king. When Brutus said he would stay away Cassius asked, 'What if they summon us?', to which Brutus replied that in that case he could not remain silent, but would be ready to die in defence of freedom. Cassius followed this up by asking what Roman would be content to let him die in such circumstances. There had been pointed inscriptions on the statue of Lucius Brutus and on that of Caesar and anonymous messages left on Brutus's praetor's tribunal which, as Cassius pointed out, showed that action was expected of him, and action worthy of his ancestors, to bring an end to tyranny.[17] Men were ready to suffer anything for him if he would do what they expected of him. Brutus was won over. He took on the leadership and it was he who persuaded his kinsman Decimus Brutus to take part. Decimus had first been approached by Cassius but would not commit himself until he had had an interview with Marcus and satisfied himself that he was the leader of the enterprise.

Next in Plutarch's account comes the story of how Porcia was let into the secret. She observed how preoccupied and worried her husband was and saw that he had something on his mind. So she decided to prove to herself that she was fit to share the secret. She took a small sharp knife and made a deep cut in her thigh. When Brutus saw her in pain and was naturally upset, she explained what she had done. Women, she said, were generally considered too weak to keep a secret. She had the advantage of being both the daughter of Cato and the wife of Brutus to counteract this natural weakness, but she had not had sufficient confidence in herself until now when she had proved to her own satisfaction that she could rise superior to pain. She then showed Brutus the wound. He was astonished, and raising his hands to heaven prayed that he might succeed in his undertaking and so prove himself a worthy husband of Porcia.[18] She did not in fact prove quite so strong-willed as this incident suggests. When the Ides of March came she worked herself up into a frenzy of excitement, kept sending messages to the forum, and finally collapsed.

The fifteenth of March, the Ides, had been chosen as the day when Caesar was to be killed because a Senate meeting had been fixed for that day, and there was every reason to expect Caesar's presence at it. He was soon to set out on a new campaign, against the Parthians, and at the Senate meeting, so it was believed, an announcement was to be made that according to the Sibylline books the Parthians could only be conquered by a king and a proposal would therefore be put that the title of king should be conferred on Caesar. This, according to Cicero, was a false rumour, but it may none the less have been believed, and have encouraged the conspirators to do the deed before they were put in the embarrassing situation of having to express an opinion on the proposal.[19] The meeting was to take place in a room in the complex of buildings surrounding the theatre of Pompey, and when the day came Brutus set out with his dagger, while the rest assembled at Cassius's house and went from there to the meeting. There were some anxious moments. Harmless remarks were interpreted as evidence that the secret had leaked. Caesar was late in arriving; whether because of his wife's forebodings or because he was in poor health, he was doubtful whether to come until he yielded to Decimus Brutus's persuasions. But in the end all went according to plan. Caesar lay dead at the foot of Pompey's statue with twenty-three wounds in his body.

The conspiracy had succeeded. In a way it had been too easy. Caesar was not the typical tyrant as depicted by the ancients, surrounded by his bodyguard, suspicious and fearful. For all his autocratic behaviour he belonged to the free and open society of the Roman Republic. His approachability and his carelessness for his safety made it fairly easy to kill him. At the same time it weakened the moral case of the conspirators, and made it less easy to follow up the assassination. There was no case for a coup d'état. The conspirators had no plans for action apart from killing Caesar. They were the champions of constitutionalism and their idea was that once Caesar was out of the way the constitution would automatically be restored and would operate on its own. And the fact that Caesar had destroyed relatively little made this seem more plausible. The old organs of government had not been abolished. There were still consuls and praetors, though they owed their positions to Caesar's favour; the Senate still met, though it had lost its prestige and its freedom of speech. For all the irregularities and the lack of real freedom, the constitution still existed.

Why was the conspiracy, so successfully executed, so sad a failure in its results? One answer would be that the conspirators were not sufficiently ruthless. At the time of his death Caesar held the dual position of consul and dictator. As consul he had as colleague Mark Antony; as dictator his second-in-command (Master of the Horse) was M. Aemilius Lepidus. Lepidus was not a man of much weight, but Antony with his vigorous personality and popular gifts was more formidable, and the question was whether he should be killed at the same time as Caesar. Most of the conspirators wanted to do so, and Cicero, wise after the event and more bloodthirsty perhaps than he would have been at the time, maintained that this was what he would have done if he had been one of them. Brutus, however, would have none of this and his view prevailed. It is to his credit that he was against unnecessary bloodshed, but his hopes that Antony would have a change of heart and would assist in the re-establishment of freedom were perhaps a little naive. As it was, Antony was taken aside by Trebonius, one of the conspirators, and kept out of the way while Caesar was being despatched.

Another answer to the question why the conspiracy was ultimately a failure would be that Brutus and the others did not act with sufficient vigour after the deed was done. Cicero, and others too, maintained that they should have summoned the Senate, stirred up popular enthusiasm more vigorously, and assumed the leadership of the whole commonwealth.[20] He may have been right; he himself was later to show what could be done even by one holding no office. But Brutus, respected though he was, lacked popular gifts, and was, it seems, rather slow to move. Moreover he was not the sole leader. Cassius was the older man and had more experience, and the two seem to have agreed to exercise a kind of joint leadership which cannot have been conducive to effective action. In any case it is doubtful whether they would ever have had the requisite popular support. However much the Republic might mean to the Roman nobles who had held or might expect to hold its offices, it meant little to the Roman people as a whole. Then there was the army, or rather the armies. The conspirators had no armed force behind them and they could hardly expect the loyalties of Caesar's veterans to be transferred to his murderers. Finally there was Caesar's heir to be taken into account, the young Octavius, to whom no one gave a thought when the assassination was planned. As things turned out the result of Caesar's death was a dismal period of civil war and uneasy peace which ended only in 31 BC with the battle of Actium. Caesar's heir became ruler of the Roman world, and as time went on the relics of republican government faded away in the face of increasing autocracy.

Brutus had raised his dagger and struck Caesar with the others; his hand had also been accidentally wounded by the dagger of one of the other assassins, so that he must have presented a particularly bloody spectacle as he went out with the others, dagger in hand, calling on the people of Rome to assert their freedom. It was an old established Roman custom for magistrates to keep the general public informed by summoning meetings in the forum, and the conspirators would naturally wish to explain their action to the people of Rome. One account makes them go at once to the forum and calm the excited populace by an exposition of their motives and intentions.[21] If they did make formal speeches at this stage, they cannot have had much success in reassuring the people, for all accounts agree that they were forced to take refuge on the Capitol. Probably it was only later in the day, when Brutus and Cassius were brought down to the forum from the Capitol, that the two leaders obtained a hearing.[22] They were listened to respectfully, but they failed to make much of an impression and went back to spend the night on the Capitol.

The next day there was another public speech by Brutus, this time on the Capitol. It was carefully prepared; or, if not, it was revised and polished afterwards, for some two months later Brutus arranged for its publication, sending it first to Cicero for criticism. Cicero found it excellent of its kind, but Brutus's kind was not his. It could not have been more elegantly expressed, 'but I would have put more fire into it'.[23] As the speech was published it may well be that its substance is preserved by Appian, who puts into Brutus's mouth a speech which has two main themes. First he is concerned to defend himself for having broken the oath of allegiance to Caesar which the senators had sworn; he claims that no oath can bind Romans to a tyrant and that duty to their country had over-ridden their obligations to Caesar. Second, he addresses Caesar's veterans in conciliatory terms, confirming their promised grants of land but condemning the policy of dispossessing existing holders without compensation.[24] If Brutus in fact spoke on these lines one can well believe that even though the speech met with approval, as Appian says it did, it fell short of arousing enthusiasm. He did not quite rise to the occasion.

Cicero had not been inactive on the Ides of March. Brutus recognized him as a leader in the cause of republican freedom when he called out his name as he brandished his dagger after the deed was done. Later in the day Cicero had gone up to the Capitol to urge Brutus and Cassius as praetors to summon the Senate on the spot.[25] They had not responded. The Senate did meet two days after the Ides, but it was summoned by Antony. He had at first taken refuge in his house and barricaded himself in, but he soon realized that he was in no danger. On the evening of the sixteenth, the day after the Ides, he was in confident and aggressive mood, and Decimus Brutus was already suggesting to Brutus and Cassius that they should leave Italy.[26] Antony was indeed in a strong position. As a close associate of Caesar he was heir to his prestige and his popularity and had access to his papers and his funds; at the same time as consul he held the highest position in the state, a position which Brutus and the rest as champions of constitutionalism were bound to respect. He played his hand skilfully; at first he was moderate and conciliatory, but it soon became apparent that he meant to have things his own way.

When the Senate met, its members were on the whole favourable to the conspirators and a general amnesty was approved to cover their action. But Antony gained an important point when he secured the confirmation of Caesar's ordinances. Moreover the Caesarians, with the consent of Brutus, anxious for peace and harmony, obtained the Senate's approval of a public funeral for Caesar and the publication of his will. This proved disastrous from the Republican point of view. The funeral was skilfully exploited by Antony, who delivered the funeral oration, and the publication of Caesar's will, with its bequests to the Roman people, added to the unpopularity of the conspirators. The initiative passed to Antony, and Brutus and Cassius thought it wise to withdraw from Rome, where they were no longer safe. Brutus, who as city praetor was not permitted to absent himself for more than ten days, had to take advantage of Antony's proposal that the law on this point should be suspended.[27]

For five months after the Ides of March Brutus remained in Italy. It was an unsatisfactory period for him, as there was little he could do to influence events short of stirring up civil war. That he would not do. He had plenty of supporters outside Rome,[28] but he had no wish to mobilize them for action and in fact issued orders disbanding them. The only result of Caesar's assassination, Cicero wrote to Atticus in the middle of May, seemed to be that Brutus was staying on his country estate at Lanuvium while all Caesar's actions, writings, words, promises and thoughts had greater force than if he himself were alive.[29] Cicero was not in close touch with him after his departure from Rome, though he saw him at Lanuvium at the end of May.[30] Brutus relied much more on Atticus. Although he was so much older, says Cornelius Nepos, Atticus was his closest associate during this period; he was his chief adviser as well as the man he saw most of socially. Atticus was helpful and reliable and prudent, but he was not the man to inspire bold action, and he was himself by no means certain what was the best course. When a suggestion was made that the members of the equestrian order should subscribe to a fund for the republicans and that Atticus should be the first subscriber, he declined; Brutus, he said, could draw on his resources as far as they allowed, but he would not enter into any joint arrangement with others. There are some grounds for thinking that he had doubts about Brutus's leadership; at any rate we find him expressing disagreement with Cicero's view that the Republic depended on him.[31]

Cicero was no more active than Brutus. He kept away from Rome and reflected gloomily that though the tyrant was dead the tyranny was still alive.[32] At times things looked brighter. Antony's colleague in the consulship was Dolabella, who had taken Caesar's place, and at the end of April, while Antony was absent in South Italy, he showed a short-lived zeal for Republicanism which raised Cicero's spirits for a time. He took firm action against Caesarian rioters and removed a column, or altar, erected in the forum in honour of Caesar. These actions were greeted with enthusiasm by Cicero, who sent off a rather fulsome letter of congratulation to Dolabella, and wrote to Atticus that it looked as if Brutus could now walk through the forum wearing a golden crown. His experience of Dolabella as son-in-law should have taught him not to expect too much of him. Brutus was less optimistic, and wrote to Cicero that he was considering exile.[33]

On 9 May Cicero was writing that if Brutus did not go to Rome for a Senate meeting which was due to take place at the beginning of June he would never do anything in public life. But later when Brutus asked his advice, probably on whether to attend this meeting, he confessed himself unable to give any guidance.[34] At the end of May Brutus and Cassius wrote to Antony a letter which shows how weak their position was. They referred to the information they had received of a large body of veterans having come to Rome and the prospect of more being there on 1 June.

It would be quite unlike us to have any doubts or fears regarding you, but undoubtedly after we put ourselves at your disposal and in accordance with your advice dismissed our friends from the provincial towns and did this by letter as well as by edict, we deserve to share your counsels, especially in a matter which concerns us. We therefore ask you to inform us of your intentions towards us, whether you think we shall be safe among all those veterans who, we have been told, are considering replacing the altar [the memorial to Caesar which Dolabella had taken down], an action which scarcely anyone who wants us to enjoy safety and honour could desire or approve. That our aim from the beginning was peace and that we sought nothing other than the liberty of the community is clear from what has happened. There is no one who can fail us but you. Assuredly your goodness and trustworthiness make that impossible, but no one else has the capacity to deceive us, because we have trusted and will trust in you alone. Our friends are extremely alarmed about us. They are assured of your trustworthiness but they cannot help reflecting that the crowds of veterans can be stirred up by others more easily than they can be restrained by you. We ask for a reply on all these points. It is an altogether trivial and worthless claim to allege that the veterans have been summoned because you were going to bring forward a motion about their interests in June. Who do you think will stand in the way of that, when you know well that we will keep quiet? Nobody ought to think us too eager for life when nothing can happen to us without universal destruction and ruin.[35]

What reply if any was made to this letter we do not know. The writers did not go to Rome.

The next development was a decision by the Senate to give Brutus and Cassius the job of purchasing corn in Asia and Sicily respectively. They were to be granted provinces in due course, as could be expected by praetors; in the meantime the corn commission was a device, and a somewhat humiliating one, for getting them out of the way.[36] Cicero now went over to Antium on the coast of Latium (modern Anzio), where Brutus and Cassius and others were assembled, with the wives of the two Republican leaders and Brutus's mother. Cicero was asked his advice by Brutus and was urging him to accept the corn commission, on the ground that his safety was paramount, when Cassius came in and 'looking valiant, the living image of Mars', said he would not go to Sicily; 'Am I the man to accept an insult as if it was a favour?' He proposed to go to Greece, and Brutus, when asked by Cicero what he intended, said he would go to Rome if Cicero agreed. Cicero would only agree if Brutus was likely to be safe and that he did not think would be the case. There was much talk about their missed opportunities, but when Cicero began to tell the company what ought to have been done he was cut short by Servilia indignantly exclaiming, 'I've never heard anything like it'. The upshot of the meeting was that Brutus gave up the idea of going to Rome; both he and Cassius seemed likely to leave Italy, and Servilia, who still had, or thought she had, influence with the Caesarians, promised to get the corn commission removed from the Senate decree. Cicero felt that his visit had been pretty futile. He had found, as he put it in a letter to Atticus, the ship going to pieces, or rather its pieces scattered. 'No plan, no thought, no method.'[37]

Brutus set out from Antium on 25 June, but he proceeded very slowly 'in case something should turn up'. On 8 July he was staying at Nesis, an island in the bay of Naples, and he had not got much further over a month later, on 17 August, when Cicero met him at Velia in Lucania.[38] One reason for his tardiness, at any rate initially, was his anxiety about the reaction to the *ludi Apollinares*, which took place on 6 to 13 July. As city praetor he was responsible for these shows, and although he was unable to be present in person his hope was that the occasion would provide proof of his popularity. Atticus helped with the arrangements and was in Rome to report on how things went, but Cicero was unable to agree to Brutus's suggestion that he too should attend, a suggestion which he thought showed a lack of Brutus's usual good sense.[39] It was mortifying to Brutus that the games were announced as taking place in *July*, the new name for the month which should have lapsed with the death of the Julius whom it commemorated, and the Greek shows which formed part of the programme were poorly attended; but a play by the tragedian Accius, the *Tereus*, was the occasion for gratifying demonstrations. These may not have been quite so enthusiastic as Cicero later represented them to be, but they certainly showed that Brutus had a following in Rome, though as Cicero put it at the time it was a pity the Romans should use their hands in clapping rather than in defending the Republic.[40]

Towards the end of July Brutus and Cassius issued an edict, or manifesto, which Cicero described as very reasonable. It was evidently meant to be conciliatory and contained an offer to withdraw from Italy and an undertaking not to provide any occasion for civil war.[41] It produced a reply from Antony, in the form both of a public edict and of a private letter, which Brutus and Cassius found insulting and threatening. They made a firm and dignified reply in which they protested against the threats of force which their offer had produced.

You must realize that it is intolerable that praetors should not be allowed to relinquish their rights in the interests of peace and freedom without being threatened with armed force; it is not right or proper for us to be submissive nor should Antony expect to give orders to those to whom he owes his freedom. If we had other inducements to stir up civil war your letter would have no effect; threats have no force with free men; but you understand perfectly well that we cannot be driven in any direction, and perhaps you take up this threatening attitude to make our deliberate plan look like fear. Our view is this. We want you to hold a high and honourable position in a free republic and we have no desire to enter into hostilities with you; but we value our freedom above your friendship. We beg you to consider what you are undertaking and what is within your powers, and to consider not how long Caesar lived but for how short a time he was king. We pray that your counsels may be beneficial to the commonwealth and to yourself; if not, our hope is that they may harm you as little as possible while the safety and honour of the commonwealth are unimpaired.

Very well written, said Cicero, but 'what the effect of these edicts is and what they hope to achieve I cannot see.'[42]

Cicero himself had after long hesitation decided to leave Italy until the end of the year, when the new consuls would take office. He wanted to see his son, who was studying at Athens and in need of some parental supervision; apart from that he found it hard to decide between the claims of prudence which suggested that it was safer for him to go and those of duty to his country, which he might still be able to serve. In the event things were to some extent decided for him. He set out from the south of Italy and was driven back by adverse winds, winds which he later compared to patriotic fellow citizens who refused to allow him to desert the Republic.[43] Then he heard of Brutus's conciliatory edict and was given some over-optimistic news of the prospects; according to his informants there were hopes of a compromise, of a change of heart on the part of Antony, of Brutus and Cassius returning to Rome. He learnt too that people were criticizing him for his absence.[44] He had been none too happy about leaving the country, and this decided him. He at once changed his plans and decided to go to Rome. On his way back he met Brutus at Velia and there learnt that the situation was by no means as favourable as he had been given to understand. But Brutus was delighted with his decision and gave him every encouragement to persist in it. And so Cicero, whom the conspirators had left out because they thought him too old and too timid, returned to Rome to take up the fight for freedom, while the hero of the Ides of March left the country after some months of inglorious inactivity. He was followed shortly after by Cassius.[45]

Porcia had accompanied Brutus to Velia, and in the house where they stayed was a picture of Hector's farewell to Andromache before he went out to battle. It showed Hector handing their child to his wife while Andromache had her eyes on her husband, and Porcia could not help weeping as she looked at the scene. Brutus and a friend of his exchanged quotations from the passage in Homer that had inspired the picture. The friend repeated the lines in which Andromache described Hector as father, mother and brother to her as well as husband. Brutus smiled and quoted the line in which Hector told his wife to attend to her loom and distaff, but only to say that this was inappropriate to Porcia, whose body might be that of a weak woman but whose spirit was as staunch in the cause of her country as that of her menfolk.[46]

Brutus's departure into voluntary exile was a confession of failure. He might well have felt depressed and humiliated. But if we can believe Cicero he had no such feelings, or if he did he did not show them. He was sustained by the consciousness of the glorious deed he had done and any sorrow he felt at leaving was on behalf of Rome, not of himself.[47] He was not the man to be afflicted with doubts about the rightness of his action.

4 BRUTUS IN THE EAST

Something must now be said about political developments in the period from the Ides of March to the departure of Brutus and Cassius. First the provincial appointments. Two of the conspirators, Decimus Brutus and Trebonius, had been appointed to provinces for the current year but had not yet taken up their appointments; they now left Rome, Decimus Brutus for Cisalpine Gaul and Trebonius for Asia. Lepidus, who had been allotted Gallia Narbonensis and Nearer Spain, had also not yet left Rome; after Antony had secured for him the honorific post of *pontifex maximus*, previously held by Caesar, he departed for his provinces. For the next year, 43, Antony had his eyes on Macedonia, where there were a number of Roman legions, ready for Caesar's projected expedition against the Parthians, which he wanted to have under his control. He allotted Macedonia to himself, while Dolabella, whose anti-Caesarian feelings proved short-lived, was awarded Syria.[1]

Soon however Antony changed his mind. He decided to take Cisalpine and Transalpine Gaul instead of Macedonia and to have the Macedonian legions transferred to him in Italy. Early in June, unable to get senatorial approval, he got a law passed by the assembly giving him the Gallic provinces for five years. It was all too reminiscent of Caesar. As for Brutus and Cassius, the corn commission which they were given in June did not, as we have seen, preclude their being allotted provinces for 43, and in July or at the beginning of August it was decided that Brutus should have Crete and Cassius Cyrenaica. Both were unimportant provinces and they ignored the decision.

The most important development, though it may not have been recognized as such at the time, was the arrival in Italy of Caesar's great-nephew Octavius, the future emperor Augustus. He was a young man of eighteen completing his education at Apollonia in Illyria when the news reached him of his great-uncle's death. On arrival in Italy he learnt that under Caesar's will he was made heir to three-quarters of his property and was adopted as his son. He decided to accept the inheritance, and acceptance for him entailed the obligation to avenge his adoptive father's death. In mid-April he arrived in Naples and met Cicero, who was favourably impressed by him personally, but feared the influence of those around him.[2] Nor was his arrival welcome to Antony, who had himself hoped to be Caesar's heir and son by adoption, and who found his position endangered by the presence of a rival and one who was a mere boy. Antony treated him with no respect and did his utmost to thwart him. Octavius, however, or Octavian as he became when the formalities of his adoption were completed, went about his business of strengthening his position, was well received by Caesar's veterans and by the populace of Rome, and towards the end of July celebrated the games which were due in honour of Caesar's victory at Thapsus.

We now come to the point at which Cicero returned to Rome. On 2 September he attended the Senate and delivered the speech which he published as the First Philippic. This, though moderate in tone, produced a violent rejoinder from Antony, which provoked Cicero to write his furious onslaught on him in the form of a speech, the Second Philippic. He did not publish this at the time of writing, but none the less it showed him committed to a position from which there could be no withdrawal. Antony became more and more aggressive. He erected a statue to Caesar with the inscription 'To our father and benefactor' (*parenti optimo merito*), which, as Cicero complained, had the effect of branding the liberators as parricides; and in a speech on 2 October he referred to them in terms appropriate to traitors and suggested they had been inspired by Cicero.[3] On 9 October he left Rome to take command of the four legions that had arrived at Brundisium from Macedonia, and shortly after Cicero retired to the country. The struggle was now between Antony and Octavian, the latter supported by the constitutionalists. It turned in Octavian's favour when two legions went over to him from Antony, and at the end of November Antony left Rome for Cisalpine Gaul, where he hoped to establish a strong position for himself with the legions under his command before he took over the province from Decimus Brutus at the beginning of 43. Cicero now published the Second Philippic, returned to Rome, and took up the position of leader of the Republican cause. He had in effect declared war on Antony, a war which on his side could only be waged with words.

On leaving Italy Brutus went to Athens, where he found a favourable atmosphere which must have done much to encourage him. Honorific decrees were passed by the local authorities, and statues of him and Cassius were erected on the agora close to those of Harmodius and Aristogeiton.[4] There were a number of young Romans studying in Athens, and they were strongly Republican in sentiment. Among them were Cicero's son and a young man who was later to become famous as the poet Horace. Marcus Cicero, in this respect a loyal son of his father, impressed Brutus by his hatred of tyranny; Horace was not perhaps by nature the man to give himself to a cause, but he too caught the infection. To all appearances, however, Brutus had abandoned politics and resumed the study of philosophy. He was to be seen at the lectures of the Academic Theomnestus and of Cratippus, a Peripatetic whom

Cicero considered the leading philosopher of the day and chose as his son's tutor in philosophy.[5]

According to Plutarch, while ostensibly studying philosophy Brutus was secretly preparing for war.[6] It is, however, unlikely that war was in his mind when he first came to Athens. He had withdrawn from Italy in the interests of peace, and it would be some time before he made up his mind to resort to arms. According to Cicero, speaking in the Senate in February 43, he bided his time. 'As long as he saw you were ready to put up with anything he showed a remarkable patience; after he realized that you were prepared to assert your freedom he made ready forces in support of your freedom.'[7] If we date a revival of the spirit of freedom, as Cicero did, from his speech in the Senate on 20 December, it would seem that it was only towards the end of the year that Brutus began his martial preparations.[8]

Cicero was not in close touch with him in the months that followed his departure from Italy. At the end of October neither Cicero nor Atticus had heard anything about his plans. Cicero was then hoping to hear something from Servilia, who was expecting a secret visit from Scaptius (presumably the man whom we have already met in connection with the Salaminian loan).[9] He promises to pass on anything he hears to Atticus, but there is nothing relevant in the letters of the next few weeks, and there is no evidence that Cicero was in correspondence with Brutus during the rest of the year. Brutus must have been kept informed of developments at home, but it looks as if he acted very much on his own and there was little coordination between him and the Republicans in Italy. Cicero makes no mention of him in the Third Philippic, his speech to the Senate of 20 December. His thoughts then and at the beginning of the next year were all on the other Brutus and the situation in Italy.

Then early in February an official despatch arrived informing the Senate that Brutus was in control of Macedonia, Illyria and Greece. His first step had been to send a representative to Macedonia to get in touch with the governor Hortensius (son of the famous orator and a relative of Brutus) and persuade him to hand over the province to him. This move was successful, and he received a further accession of strength when M. Appuleius, quaestor of Asia, and

Antistius Vetus, quaestor of Syria, handed over to him the money and other valuables which they were transporting to Rome. One legion which had been left behind in Macedonia was now his, and he enrolled a number of former soldiers of Pompey who were still in Greece. At Demetrias in Thessaly were some ships, arms and money which had been destined for use in Caesar's campaign against the Parthians, and these Brutus appropriated.[10] The Roman students in Athens provided him with some officers who might be inexperienced but whose loyalty could be relied on. Horace, though he was to serve as *tribunus militum* at Philippi, was hardly a natural soldier, but Cicero's son, who at the age of seventeen had commanded a cavalry squadron at Pharsalus, was a useful accession to Brutus's forces; he was sent to Macedonia to take over the legion there and he did good service on later occasions.

When Brutus was established in Macedonia he learnt that C. Antonius, brother of Mark Antony, had arrived in Illyria. His brother had engineered his appointment as governor of Macedonia on 28 November, before leaving for Cisalpine Gaul, and he had set out to take over the province. Brutus realized that his whole position would be threatened if Antonius could establish himself in Illyria with the troops which were there under the governor Vatinius. He acted at once. He marched through difficult country and in snowstorms to Dyrrhachium and thence to Apollonia. In both places the troops came over to his side. Gaius had to retreat. He fought unsuccessful engagements with Brutus and with young Cicero; finally he and his armies surrendered. Brutus had shown remarkable vigour; his success had been rapid and, as Cicero said both publicly and privately, unexpected.[11]

In the Senate Cicero proposed a motion congratulating Brutus, giving him overriding powers over Macedonia, Illyricum and Greece, confirming him in the command of the armies he had collected and authorizing him to take all necessary measures for their maintenance.[12] In the course of a stirring speech he dismissed the fears that some had expressed that the veterans might object to Brutus having an army under him.

We are trying to burst the bonds of slavery; are we to be stopped because someone says the veterans don't like it? Are there not thousands prepared to take up arms for the cause of freedom? Is there no man besides the veteran soldiers who is stirred by honest indignation to fight against slavery? . . . Finally, for I cannot hold back the words of truth and honour, if we senators are to be guided by the whims of the veterans, and all our words and deeds are to be determined by their wishes, we can only pray for death, which Romans have always preferred to servitude.[13]

These were brave words, but the fears about the veterans were all too well grounded.

Moreover it could not be denied that Brutus himself had acted without authority. What legal right had he to the position he had won for himself by force? Cicero's answer was that all Roman armies belonged to the Republic; admittedly C. Antonius had been appointed to the province of Macedonia, but as an enemy of the Republic he had no right to its armies. In fact the party of constitutionalism was finding itself in a position where it had to approve what was unconstitutional. The Republican leaders in the east were acting on their own. As Cicero observed when the news came that Cassius had got control of Syria, Brutus and Cassius had already been their own Senate on many occasions and had regarded the safety and freedom of their country as the highest law. 'Did Brutus wait for our decrees when he knew our wishes? He did not go to his own province of Crete; he hurried to Macedonia which was not his; he considered all to be his that you would wish to be yours.' In the same way Cassius, so Cicero claimed, was justified by the law of nature, the law of Jupiter himself, according to which everything beneficial to the Republic was lawful and right. 'For law is nothing other than right reason, derived from the divine power, enjoining good action and forbidding bad'.[14] This is the Stoic doctrine of natural law, but misinterpreted in a way which one might be inclined to call cynical if it were not for the lofty tone which pervades the Philippics. Cicero was sure that right was on his side. In another age he and Brutus would have claimed that they were doing the Lord's work. As it was it was virtue in the abstract that inspired them. Cicero had shed those doubts which he had expressed in the Tusculans about the power of virtue to overcome human weakness. Death, as he said in one of the Philippics, awaited all men, but virtue could deprive it of all bitterness. 'All else is illusory, uncertain, transitory and fleeting; virtue alone is secured by the deepest roots, and no force can ever shake it, none can ever dislodge it.'[15]

The extant correspondence between Cicero and Brutus extends from the end of March to the end of July of 43 BC. These were difficult months, during which the high hopes of Cicero and the Republicans faded. Decimus Brutus had refused to give up Cisalpine Gaul to Antony and was besieged by him at Mutina. With the support of Cicero and the Senate the consuls for 43, Hirtius and Pansa, set out with Octavian to relieve Decimus; they defeated Antony, but both consuls lost their lives in or as a result of the engagement. Antony succeeded in escaping with the remains of his army. He was not pursued, and was able to join Lepidus in Gaul across the Alps. The deaths of Hirtius and Pansa left Rome without consuls and Octavian in command of their forces as well as his own. The Senate might declare Antony a public enemy, but they could not rely on the armies and their commanders to continue the fight. Lepidus joined Antony and others followed. Octavian was no longer the dutiful young man nursed by Cicero to be the servant of the Republic. He was his own master, conscious of his strength, and he determined to have the consulship. He was of course far below the legal age for holding it and the Senate would not agree. He marched on Rome and resistance collapsed.

During this difficult period there were, not surprisingly perhaps, some differences of opinion between Brutus and Cicero. First there was the question of how to deal with Gaius Antonius after he had surrendered. Brutus, though himself inclined to lenient treatment, wrote to Cicero for his advice. Cicero sent an interim reply suggesting the postponement of any decision until news came of the outcome at Mutina. Then a little later things were complicated by the arrival of a despatch from Brutus, accompanied by one from Antonius in which he described himself as proconsul. When this was read out in the Senate there was consternation among the senators, for not only was Gaius brother of Mark Antony but after Antony's departure from Rome the Senate had revoked his appointment. Brutus had apparently allowed him to give himself the title of proconsul and one of Brutus's supporters was reduced to arguing that the letter was a forgery. There was a feeling that he was not being sufficiently tough. Opinion in Rome was in favour of dealing severely with those who would themselves show no mercy to the defeated. Cicero shared this opinion and expressed it to Brutus, though not very forcibly. 'If you don't agree with this point of view I shall defend your opinion without abandoning my own; men expect from you neither laxity nor cruelty; it is easy to steer a middle course – severity towards the leaders, liberality towards the men.'[16]

The argument went on. Brutus, who seems to have thought that some accommodation with the other side was still possible, maintained that it was more important to prevent civil war than to vent one's anger on the defeated. Cicero replied that severity could be salutary while leniency only encouraged civil war and that opinion in Rome was in favour of the severest punishment for those who took up arms against their country.[17] Brutus now took a strictly constitutional line. It was for the Senate and people to decide and he would not anticipate their decision. He was however convinced that he was doing right in keeping Antonius alive and in honourable captivity. 'I hold it to be much more honourable and more in accordance with the principles of the Republic not to persecute the unfortunate in adversity than to go on endlessly exciting the greed and arrogance of powerful men.' The Senate did in fact declare all the followers of Mark Antony to be enemies, and this could be interpreted to include his brother; but there seems to have been no specific decision on Gaius and Brutus kept him alive.[18] His action has been condemned as a dishonourable attempt to make friends with the Antonians.[19] Others will prefer his humanity to the vindictiveness of those in Rome, and if he had some hopes of coming to terms with Mark Antony this is not necessarily to be condemned. In the end Gaius had to be killed; but that was some months later when he had been found trying to raise a mutiny in Brutus's army and the situation in Rome had completely changed.[20]

Then there was the question of Lepidus's children. At the end of June, after he had joined with Antony, Lepidus was declared a public enemy. His wife was Brutus's half-sister, and Brutus was naturally anxious that her children should not suffer from the misdeeds of their father. At first Cicero was obdurate. He admitted that it might seem unfair to visit the sins of fathers on children, but claimed that Lepidus's unpatriotic behaviour meant that it was he who was cruel to his children rather than those who declared him a public enemy. He pointed to the precedent of Themistocles and his children in Greece, and to the penalties suffered at Rome by the offspring of those condemned in the courts. But he soon abandoned this point of view and even spoke on behalf of the children in the Senate. His change of mind he attributed to his affection for Brutus, but one suspects that he was also influenced by the appeals of Servilia, not to mention the growing weakness of the Republican position.[21]

The most serious disagreement between the two men was about Octavian. Brutus did not at all approve of Cicero's trustful attitude towards him. His earliest criticism comes in a letter of mid-May where he expresses the fear that the honours conferred on Octavian would only encourage him to aim higher. A month or so later he expressed his views at much greater length and with greater force in a letter to Atticus which has been preserved with Cicero's correspondence, presumably because Atticus passed it on to him.[22] Atticus had told Brutus that Cicero was surprised at his failure to comment on his actions, and in response to Atticus's request Brutus explained his views:

I know Cicero has done everything with the best intentions; for I have every reason to be assured of his patriotic spirit. But in some respects he seems to me to have acted – how shall I put it – amateurishly for a man of his political wisdom, or should I say presumptuously, in not hesitating to incur in behalf of the Republic the enmity of a man as powerful as Antony. There is only one thing I think I can say to you: the boy's [Octavian's] greed and ambition have been stimulated rather than checked by Cicero.

After unkindly touching on one of Cicero's weak spots, his harping on the achievements of his consulship, Brutus goes on:

Our friend Cicero boasts to me that though a civilian he has carried on the war against Antony. What, I ask, do we gain from this, if the price of crushing Antony is the acceptance of another in Antony's place, and if the man who destroys that evil is found encouraging another likely to have stronger foundations and deeper roots, if we allow it. So that it is now doubtful whether those actions of his show fear of what constitutes despotism or only of a particular despot, Antony. For my part I do not thank a man who, provided he does not serve an angry master is prepared to put up with the actual fact of slavery. And when it comes to a triumph, pay for his troops, and constant decrees encouraging him unashamedly to aim at the position of the man whose name he has taken, is this worthy of an ex-consul, or of Cicero? I could not keep silent, and what you will read will inevitably be unwelcome to you. I myself am conscious of how painful it is to have written this to you, and I know what your views are about the Republic and how little hope you have of its recovery, and I certainly don't blame you, Atticus; your age, your way of life and your children make you lacking in energy . . .

We are too much afraid of death and exile and poverty; it seems to me that Cicero thinks these the worst of ills, and provided there are those from whom he will get what he wants and who will show him respect and give him praise, he does not disdain servitude, provided it is accompanied by honours – if that is possible in the worst and most wretched state of degradation. So Octavius may call Cicero father, consult him on everything, praise him, thank him, but it will be clear all the same that his words are contradicted by his deeds. For what can be more inconsistent with ordinary human feeling than to treat as a father one who is not even reckoned as a free man? And yet the aim and object of that excellent man, the goal to which he hurries, is that Octavius should be gracious to him. For my part I set no store by those gifts which are preeminently Cicero's; what is the use of his numerous writings on freedom for the fatherland, honour, death, exile, poverty? . . . He should stop making our troubles worse by his boasts. What good is it to us that Antony has been defeated, if his defeat only leaves his place open for another to take? Long live Cicero, as he can do, cringing and subservient, if he is not ashamed of his age and his honours and his achievements; for my part the conditions of servitude could never be so favourable as to stop me from waging war against the reality, I mean against tyranny and extraordinary commands and despotism and power that sets itself above the laws, even though Octavius may be a good man, as you say he is, though I have never thought so; but it was the view of our ancestors that no one, not even a father, should have absolute power.

If I was not as fond of you as Cicero thinks Octavius is of him, I would not have written this to you. I am sorry to think of the annoyance it will cause to a man like you who is so devoted to all his friends and to Cicero in particular; but you can be assured that my personal feeling for him is unaltered, though my opinion of his judgment is very decidedly altered, and it is impossible to stop each man holding whatever opinion he has formed about something.

To Cicero himself Brutus wrote in even stronger terms in a letter probably dating from July 43.[23] This was occasioned by a letter from Cicero to Octavian, an extract from which had been sent to Brutus by Atticus. Cicero had told Octavian 'there was one thing demanded and expected of him, that he should desire the safety of those of whom right thinking Romans and the people in general thought well', that is, of Brutus and the other liberators. To Brutus this seemed like a servile appeal to a tyrant and he gave vent to his indignation in a long, repetitive and rather disagreeable letter:

Your concern for me and your care for my safety, though welcome, are no novelty. It is the regular thing, almost a daily occurrence, to hear from you of words and deeds showing your loyalty and respect for my position. But I could not have been more deeply offended by what you said in that part of your letter to Octavius about me and my friends. The way in which you thank him for his services to the Republic, the humility and subservience – I hesitate to write this, so ashamed am I of the state into which we have fallen, but yet I must – with which you commend our safety to him – worse surely than any death – make it clear that the despotism has not been got rid of, only the despot changed. Look at your own words again and dare to deny that these appeals are those of a subject to a king.

And so it goes on, at considerable length. The letter is painful to read, with its self-righteous protestations and its wounding references to Cicero's supposed desire for life at any cost.

I am not the sort of man who would ever be a suppliant, and I would go further than that, I would stop anyone who expected others to be his suppliants; if this is impossible, I shall keep away from those who are willing to be slaves, and shall judge Rome to be for me wherever it is possible to be free, and I shall pity you and your friends when neither your age nor your distinction nor the virtue of others can diminish in you the feeling that life is sweet.

The virtue of others. Brutus meant his own virtue and that of the other tyrannicides. Yet it was he who left Italy and Cicero who stayed behind. Cicero did not answer this letter. He did, however, write at some length in reply to earlier criticisms. He claimed that all the honours decreed to Octavian had been deserved and neces- sary in the circumstances, since until Decimus Brutus proved himself he had been the only person who could free Rome from Antony. He took the opportunity to review events since the Ides of March, and recalled how he had abandoned his project of leaving Italy. 'I saw you at Velia, and I was sorely grieved; you were retiring, Brutus, I say "retiring" because our friends the Stoics say a wise man does not flee. When I reached Rome I at once opposed the criminal madness of Antony. After I had aroused his wrath against me I began to put in train a plan for freeing the Republic surely worthy of a Brutus – for this sort of thing is peculiar to your family.'[24] There is an implied criticism of Brutus here, but it is expressed with a tact completely absent from Brutus's criticisms of Cicero.

It is easy to criticize at a distance, and it is easy to be uncompromising at a distance. Both Cicero and Brutus when not personally involved thought the other too conciliatory. Just as Cicero had held that Brutus's lenience to Antony had only resulted in the continuance of the tyranny after the tyrant's death, so Brutus thought that thanks to Cicero's encouragement of Octavian a new tyrant had succeeded Antony. Brutus was of course right in distrusting Octavian. Events showed that Cicero's judgment had been at fault. But he certainly deserved more sympathy than he got from the absent Brutus. He was on the spot, dealing with circumstances as they arose, keeping the Republican cause alive in Rome as best he could. It was grossly unfair to suggest that he was only out for his own safety. Unwise he may have been, but he was certainly courageous in those last months. He was taking risks, and sanguine though he always was he must have known it. Brutus had no alternative policy, or if he had he did not reveal it to Cicero.

At the end of the letter to Atticus in which he gave his views on Cicero Brutus referred to the illness of his wife Porcia. The illness proved fatal. Her death gave rise to a letter of consolation from Cicero in which he looked back to his own bereavement of two years earlier and contrasted his position then with that of Brutus now.[25] He pointed out that Brutus was a public figure on whom the eyes of all were fixed. The man who had inspired everyone to greater bravery should not himself be seen to show weakness; grief he could not escape, but it must be restrained. The tone may seem a little cold and unfeeling; but then emotion and sympathy break in with the words, 'What you have lost had no equal on this earth' (id enim amisisti cui simile in terris nihil fuit). Brutus had not in fact attained to the philosophic ideal of freedom from emotion. He felt the loss of his wife deeply. There was a letter, no longer extant, known to Plutarch, in which he lamented her death and blamed his friends for not looking after her properly.[26] He may have been unfair to his friends, but at least he cannot be accused of indifference.

These are the facts about the death of Porcia. The legend is different. The common belief in antiquity was that after Brutus's death she was determined not to survive him, and when her friends kept all weapons away from her she killed herself by swallowing live coals. The story was found as early as the Augustan age, in Nicolaus of Damascus; it was repeated by Valerius Maximus and by later Greek historians and was made the subject of an epigram of Martial.[27] It is easy to understand the appeal of a story that illustrated both the conjugal fidelity and the courage of Cato's daughter. It is less easy to see how it arose, unless it was that Porcia did in fact put an end to her life by swallowing, or inhaling, live coals, and that the popular story was wrong only in dating this to after Brutus's own death. Certainly what Plutarch says could be interpreted to mean that while suffering from some illness she voluntarily chose death. On the other hand the letter, according to Plutarch, indicated her love for Brutus, and it would have been a strange way of showing that love to take her life while he was still living.

As the situation worsened in Rome, Cicero's hopes turned more and more towards Brutus. Early in June, when he was beginning to have doubts about his ability to control Octavian, he was urging Brutus to hasten to Rome and there to complete the work of liberation that he had initiated. In July, after the defection of Lepidus, he assured Brutus that even if his military aid proved unnecessary his political guidance would be required. 'Come to the rescue then, I beseech you, and as soon as possible, and be assured that your service to the fatherland on the Ides of March was no greater than will be that conferred by your speedy arrival.' Finally, on 27 July, in a despondent letter in which he has to admit that he no longer has any influence over Octavian, he reports a conference with Servilia and some friends of Brutus. She had asked Cicero's opinion whether Brutus should be summoned or whether it was better for him to wait, and Cicero had replied that he should come to the rescue as soon as possible.[28] Nothing came of these appeals.

This is the last extant letter from Cicero to Brutus, and may well have been the last he wrote to him. On 19 August Octavian was proclaimed consul, with a relative of his, a nonentity called Pedius, as colleague. Cicero gave up the struggle. A law was passed setting up a special court to try the assassins of Caesar, and Brutus and Cassius were condemned in their absence. Octavian met Antony and Lepidus and formed with them a triumvirate for 'constituting the Republic'. Then came the savage proscriptions, with Cicero as the chief victim. When the news of Cicero's death reached Brutus his comment, according to Plutarch, was that he felt shame for its cause rather than grief at the event. His shame was not for any failure on his own part, but for the feebleness of his friends at Rome, who he thought had only themselves to blame for their state of servitude.[29] This is painful to read. Cicero had been so anxious for Brutus's friendship; he had given him affection and he believed it was returned. He was mistaken. If Plutarch has reported him correctly Brutus felt no sorrow at the loss of the man with whom he had been so closely associated over the years.

5 THE END

Cassius had followed Brutus to Athens, and from there he went first to the province of Asia and then to Syria. He was well received by the Roman commanders and their forces. He was supplied with money and ships in Asia, and in Syria the governor of the province, Statius Murcus, and Marcius Crispus, governor of Bithynia, who were besieging the Caesarian Caecilius Bassus in Apamea, handed over their forces to him, whereupon Bassus surrendered and also joined Cassius. To the eight legions acquired from these sources were added four more which were on their way through Syria from Egypt. Cassius could announce to Cicero early in March 43 that he had complete control of Syria.[1] There was however a complication. Dolabella had been appointed governor of Syria, and early in the year he arrived in Asia, where he treacherously killed the governor Trebonius. The Republicans thus lost one of their leading supporters and they no longer had control of an important province. This partly explains why Brutus did not respond to Cicero's appeals to come to the rescue in Italy. Though the Senate had instructed him in February to remain as near to Italy as possible, when they heard the news of Trebonius's death they authorized him to attack Dolabella if he thought fit.[2] Early in May he moved eastward from Dyrrhachium on the Adriatic into Macedonia, and later in the month when a report reached Rome that Dolabella had sent five cohorts to the Chersonese and Brutus decided to attack them, Cicero approved his decision.[3] The report may have been a false one, but Brutus's attention was now directed to Thrace and the Hellespont. Cassius dealt successfully with Dolabella, who proceeded to Syria and after being shut out of Antioch took refuge in Laodicea, where he was besieged and finally committed suicide. But the end of the affair did not come until July.

Meanwhile Brutus consolidated his position. He crossed the Hellespont into Asia, and received a contingent of troops from Deiotarus, whom he had laid under an obligation by his speech before Caesar a few years earlier. He wrote a brusque letter demanding supplies from the people of Pergamum: 'I hear you have given money to Dolabella. If you did so voluntarily you must admit that you have done wrong; if involuntarily, prove it by giving willingly to me.'[4] Either now or at a later stage he sent an emissary to Bithynia to obtain two hundred war ships and fifty transport vessels. He used the same argument as he had used to the Pergamenes, that they should do for him what they had done for Dolabella, an argument unlikely to appeal to the victims of these exactions. The Bithynians were in fact slow in meeting Brutus's demands and he had to go on pressing them.[5]

Soon Brutus was back in Europe, winning the support of the Thracian tribes, or where necessary operating against them. His successful attack on one of these tribes, the Bessi, led to his being hailed as *imperator* by his troops, an honour which brought him new prestige as a commander and enabled him to add the title to his name on official documents and coins. It could be conferred for quite minor successes, and there is evidence that his activities in Thrace were disappointing in their results,[6] but his position there was sufficiently secure for him to cross over again to Asia towards the end of August, this time with his armies. Octavian's consulate and the passing of the law against Caesar's assassins meant that he could only look forward to armed conflict. It was essential to co-ordinate his activities with those of Cassius as well as to complete his control over Asia Minor. He proceeded down the coast. At Clazomenae, as Horace recalled in one of his satires,[7] he heard a case involving two bitter enemies, the Italian Rupilius Rex and a wealthy local business man, Persius Hybrida. Hybrida combined flattery of Brutus with abuse of Rex and finally won the war of words with a pun on his adversary's name. Brutus, he said, was in the habit of getting rid of kings; why did he not assassinate this Rex? To the reader of Horace the satire may seem one of his least effective and the incident on which it is based a trivial one. But it has some interest for the biographer of Brutus. It shows him performing the function of a provincial governor holding his assize courts; it also shows, what one might not otherwise suppose, that it was possible to make a joke, and a not very respectful one, in his presence.

Cassius had projected an expedition against Egypt, but Brutus reminded him that they must concentrate on liberating Italy and he abandoned the project. He moved north from Syria, and at the end of 43 or the beginning of the next year the two leaders met at Smyrna. The spring of 42 was occupied with extending their control over the communities of Asia Minor and obtaining more troops and money. Cassius had the task of reducing Rhodes; Brutus dealt with the Lycians in the south-west part of Asia Minor. The Lycians were organized in a confederacy, which had been given its freedom by Rome in the second century BC and still maintained its independence. With this tradition of freedom they resented Brutus's demands and resisted his armies. Resistance was eventually concentrated in the city of Xanthos. The Xanthians destroyed the houses outside the walls and surrounded the city with a trench and embankment. The Romans brought up their siege equipment and kept up a vigorous assault day and night, urged on by Brutus. The defenders made a sortie to set fire to the Roman siege engines, but the Romans, who had withdrawn under orders, made a sudden attack and inflicted heavy losses. The gates had been shut, with the result that the Xanthians were trapped outside, and so, when a second sortie was made, the gates were left open and the Romans succeeded in breaking in. The defences were breached in other places, and the siege was at an end. The people of Xanthos preferred death to surrender; they rejected Brutus's offer of terms, killed one another and burned the bodies on pyres.

Brutus now turned his attention to another Lycian city, Patara. When the inhabitants returned no answer to his demands he gave them a day for further consideration and moved forward his troops. The Patareans surrendered and were ordered to give up their gold and silver and other treasures.[8] Other Lycian communities were invited by letter to choose between the fate of the Xanthians, who had 'made their fatherland the grave of their madness', and that of the Patareans, who had entrusted themselves to him and consequently enjoyed complete freedom. In another letter he threatened those who gave refuge to any escaped Xanthians with a fate as bad as that of Xanthos itself, but he excepted from these threats the Patareans and other peoples who had not resisted, 'so that seeing what happened to the Xanthians they may realize that they were right in deciding to regard us as friends and not enemies'.[9]

The account given above of Brutus's treatment of Xanthos and Patara is that of Appian. Plutarch's version is very different. He displays Brutus as a model of generosity and humanity, and paints a pathetic picture of his efforts to save the Xanthians. In his first operations against the Lycians he had released his captives without ransom, hoping to win the people over by kindness. It was in vain; they remained obdurate and the siege of the city was therefore inevitable. When the Xanthians set fire to some Roman siege engines the wind blew the flames back to the town, and some of the houses caught fire; Brutus, anxious for the safety of the city, ordered his men to help put out the fire; but they were frustrated by the inhabitants, who not only drove off the would-be helpers but, bent on self-destruction, themselves fed the flames. Brutus rode round the city begging the people in vain to save themselves, and after hearing of one incident of self-destruction he burst into tears. Patara on the other hand was won over by kindness. Brutus released without ransom some women, wives and daughters of leading citizens; they were impressed by his generosity and persuaded their menfolk to surrender.[10]

This is a little too good to be true. No doubt Brutus would have preferred not to use force, and he may well have been genuinely distressed at the results of the Xanthians' intransigence. But they had brought it on themselves by refusing his friendship. *Parcere subiectis et debellare superbos* was the Roman principle; and the 'proud' were those who were foolish enough to resist the Romans.

About midsummer the two leaders and their armies met at Sardis. There had been a number of disagreements between them which had to be settled, and they decided to have a private meeting. It ended in a violent quarrel, which was only stopped when Favonius, a slightly ridiculous figure, a follower of Cato who went further than his model in cultivating the frankness of the Cynics, broke in. His intervention made Cassius laugh, and though Brutus was not amused the two separated, and by the evening when they dined together they were on good terms again. One ground for dissension was the strict morality of Brutus which contrasted with Cassius's more accommodating attitude. There was an example of this the very day after their quarrel. One of Brutus's friends, Lucius Pella, who had been found guilty of embezzling money at Sardis was severely punished by him, whereas only a few days before Cassius had officially acquitted two of his friends who had been similarly guilty, and had continued them in his service after a private reprimand. Cassius was annoyed at Brutus's strictness, feeling no doubt that whether intentionally or not it showed up his own connivance at irregularities. The quarrel at Sardis is not really surprising. The joint leadership inevitably imposed strains, which were accentuated by the marked and contrasting personalities of the two leaders. But their old friendship and close association was strong enough to stand the strain. They proceeded with their armies to the Hellespont.

Before they crossed over from Asia Brutus had a vision. This is the story as told by Plutarch:

He was naturally wakeful, and by practice and self-control he had reduced his sleep to the minimum. He never went to bed during the day and at night only when everyone else had retired and it was impossible to conduct business or discuss matters. On this occasion, when the war had begun and, with the conduct of the whole business in his hands, his thoughts were concentrated on the future, he would take a little sleep in the evening after eating and then devote the rest of the night to urgent matters. If he could organize the business on hand so as to despatch it quickly, he would read a book until midnight, when the centurions and tribunes used to come and see him. When he was about to bring his army across from Asia it was the depth of night, his tent was dimly lit, and the whole camp was wrapped in silence. While he was considering something and reflecting within himself, he thought he heard someone coming in. Turning his eyes towards the entrance he saw a strange unusual figure, a monstrous and fearful form, standing in silence before him. He ventured to question it, asking 'Who are you, whether man or god, and with what purpose have you come here?' The apparition answered 'I am your evil genius, Brutus. And you will see me at Philippi.' And Brutus unperturbed said 'I shall see you.'

After the apparition had left, Brutus called his slaves, who assured him that they had neither seen nor heard anything, and in the morning Cassius, whom he had informed of the vision, tried to rationalize it and explain it as due to Brutus's overwrought state.[11]

There is no authority in Plutarch for Shakespeare's identification of the apparition with the ghost of Caesar. According to one ancient writer, Valerius Maximus, Caesar's ghost appeared at Philippi, but to Cassius not to Brutus.[12] What Brutus saw was his own evil genius, and a man's evil genius is the bad, or unfortunate, side of his nature, bad judgment or simply bad luck. These were certainly with Brutus at Philippi, and the vision, or dream, or whatever it was, if it has any basis in fact, may have reflected some anxieties or doubts about his ability to meet the supreme test.

Doubts however, if he did have them, were suppressed. Even when he saw the apparition he was unmoved and ready to meet it at Philippi. He appeared confident, convinced of the rightness of his cause, though ready to face with equanimity the possibility of death. In a letter to Atticus written shortly before Philippi, a letter which unfortunately we know only from Plutarch's summary, he claimed that nothing could be nobler than the situation he was in, since he would either conquer and give freedom to the Roman people or be freed from slavery by death; the only uncertainty was whether they would live in freedom or die.[13] The coins which he issued in 43 and 42 reiterate the theme of liberty. Some of them merely bear the head of Libertas personified, but there is one, more provocative and egotistic, with Brutus's head on one side and on the other a dagger and the cap of liberty, with the inscription 'Ides of March'. This was a famous coin. It evidently made an impression in antiquity, since it is mentioned by the historian Dio; it was imitated in sixteenth-century Italy by a would-be Brutus, Lorenzino de' Medici; and in the eighteenth century a signet ring bearing its emblems, the cap, the dagger and the reference to the Ides of March, might be worn as an indication of republican sympathies.[14] There were also coins struck by Brutus which carried no political message. Some bear the head of Apollo or emblems connected with him, and this, combined with the fact that Apollo was the watchword which he gave at Philippi, suggests that he felt a particular attraction to this god.[15] The attraction was natural in a man like Brutus steeped in Greek culture. It was ironical that his enemy Octavian also, though at a later date, adopted Apollo as his special deity.

For the triumvirs constituting the Republic meant first eliminating their enemies, and with the new year (42) they began to prepare an expeditionary force to meet that of the Republicans in the East. Pompey's son Sextus, who had survived the campaign of Munda and acquired an army and a fleet, now occupied Sicily. Apart from this the triumvirs had control of the West. It was enough to leave Lepidus in Italy with three legions, while the rest of their forces under Antony and Octavian were used against Brutus and Cassius. A part of the force was sent ahead under Decidius Saxa and Norbanus Flaccus and the remainder was transported across the Adriatic in the course of the summer, moved eastwards along the Via Egnatia, and assembled at Amphipolis.

Brutus and Cassius, who had wasted valuable time on their operations against Rhodes and the Lycians, now crossed the Hellespont, to find that Saxa and Norbanus had taken up positions on the road eastwards well in advance of the main force. They succeeded however in outflanking them, and the Caesarian forces withdrew to join the main army. The Republicans advanced into Macedonia and took up a position to the west of the town of Philippi. The position was a strong one, with mountains on the right and marshy ground on the left, and they were within easy reach of the port of Neapolis, through which, with their naval forces in command of the Aegean, they could bring up supplies from their base on the island of Thasos. Brutus and Cassius had separate camps a mile or so apart on either side of the Via Egnatia, with a fortification drawn across from one camp to another.

The two armies were evenly matched as regards numbers.[16] Each was under dual control, Octavian and Antony facing Brutus and Cassius. Of the four Antony was the best general, though Cassius had wide experience of warfare and his army was well disciplined. Brutus had shown vigour and enterprise since he moved into Macedonia, but he had no real flair as a commander and the organization of his army was weak.[17] Octavian, apart from his youth and inexperience, was incapacitated by illness. He stayed at Dyrrhachium for a time, and though he eventually joined his army he was still unwell and had to be carried round reclining in a litter. None the less he contributed something which counted for much with the army, the name of Caesar. The Republican forces were better equipped than those of the Caesarians, and Brutus could afford to allow his men certain luxuries which seem out of keeping with his own philosophic highmindedness. He provided his officers with splendid armour, adorned with gold and silver, in the belief that this would encourage the ambitious and make the avaricious more eager to fight, in defence of the treasure they carried on their persons.[18]

By such material means morale was raised among those for whom it was not enough to be fighting for freedom. As for the leaders, they were confident of the justice of their cause. They were determined on victory or death. They would not survive defeat, but would rather seek freedom by voluntarily ending their lives. If we can believe Plutarch, Brutus and Cassius discussed the matter immediately before the battle. Cassius asked his friend's opinion and Brutus replied that he had changed his views since the time when he had criticized Cato for taking his own life. If he should be defeated he would not renew the struggle, but would leave this life praising fortune. 'On the Ides of March I gave my life to my country and since then I have for her sake lived another life of freedom and glory.' Cassius smiled and said, 'In this spirit let us go against the enemy. Either we shall conquer or we shall not fear the conquerors.'[19] Cassius was all too ready to carry out this decision.

It was late in the campaigning season. Winter was approaching and the Caesarians were short of supplies. From the Republicans' point of view there was much to be said for postponing an engagement, and this was the policy advocated by Cassius. Brutus, however, favoured immediate action, and his policy prevailed. According to Plutarch his motives were idealistic: the desire to free his country as soon as possible and to relieve the peoples of the burdens of war; but he was also encouraged by some successes in cavalry skirmishes, while the fear of desertions brought some of Cassius's officers round to Brutus's view. But in fact the course of events was determined more by Antony's decision to attack than by any decision on the part of Brutus.[20] Antony's first plan was to turn the flank of the Republicans and cut their communications by making a causeway across the marsh, but counterworks by Cassius's men frustrated his efforts. He led his army against the fortifications of Cassius and this provoked Brutus's army to attack.

The battle, the first of the two battles of Philippi, was a disorderly affair on the Republican side, a sad story of confusion. Brutus was on the right wing facing Octavian, Cassius on the left opposite Antony. Brutus's men attacked prematurely before he gave the word; the legions were thrown out of line and some of them were carried too far to the right. But disorderly though it was, the attack was successful. Brutus's forces routed those of Octavian and burst into his camp, from which, however, he had prudently had himself removed.[21] While Brutus was victorious Antony overwhelmed Cassius's forces in a swift and sudden attack. And here there was a lamentable, and indeed inexcusable, failure of communication between the two armies. Cassius was unaware of Brutus's success; Brutus assumed that Cassius had been successful, and when he discovered the truth it was too late for him to bring assistance.

After his forces had broken and fled Cassius retired to high ground, and when he saw a troop of Brutus's men approaching he thought they were enemies and sent one of his officers Titinius to reconnoitre. Titinius was surrounded and welcomed with enthusiasm, but Cassius watching from a distance was convinced that he had been captured by the enemy, and reproching himself bitterly retired to a tent and put an end to his life. The unfortunate Titinius, blaming himself for his slowness in returning, likewise killed himself. This is one version of Cassius's end. According to another he had already decided to kill himself when a messenger came to inform him of Brutus's victory. Cassius merely said, 'Tell him I hope his victory may be complete', and asked his shield bearer to kill him at once and deliver him from his shame.'¹

The loss of Cassius, though serious, was not disastrous. Though Brutus pronounced him 'the last of the Romans' there was still Brutus himself, and he had not lost heart. The Republicans had if anything had the best of the first engagement, and they still had the advantage of a strong position and plentiful supplies. But Cassius's men were not altogether reliable. They had lost their leader, and they resented having to fight under a different commander and one whose troops had had a success which was in marked contrast to their own failure. There were some desertions and fear of more. Brutus did his best to encourage them by words and gifts. He even promised them as a reward of victory the plunder of Thessalonica and Sparta, a promise which Plutarch, in general so favourable to Brutus, considered indefensible.²³ Brutus was forced to abandon his principles and, according to Plutarch, to follow the advice of lesser men who persuaded him that this was the only way Cassius's men could be induced to fight effectively.

The Caesarians were short of supplies and suffering from the bad weather. If Brutus could have postponed action further they might well have been in serious straits. This was in fact his policy, but his troops had been victorious once and did not see why they should be condemned to inactivity, while their opponents, anxious for immediate action, provoked them with taunts and challenges. The officers, while approving Brutus's policy in theory, thought it would be better to take advantage of the present militant spirit of the soldiers. Brutus was not like Cassius a strict disciplinarian who could impose his decisions on his officers. He gave way, saying 'I seem to be fighting the battle like Pompey, less as leader than as led'. And if we can believe Appian he did not conceal his reluctance to fight, but made, one might almost say, the worst of the situation by telling the troops as he rode round that it was they who had chosen to fight and had forced him into battle when he could have conquered by other means.²⁴

On 23 October, three weeks after the first engagement, Brutus led his army into battle. He was at first successful, but his success was only partial and short-lived. The day ended with complete victory for Antony and Octavian. Aided by one of his companions Lucilius, who claimed to be Brutus and so drew off some horsemen who were following him, Brutus escaped from the battlefield with a few companions. Among them was Publius Volumnius, a philosopher, according to Plutarch, a former fellow-student of Brutus and his companion throughout his campaigns. They came to a stream with steep wooded banks. Brutus sat down in a hollow opposite a rock, looked up at the stars (for it was by now dark) and quoted two lines of Greek. One was from Euripides's *Medea*, 'Zeus, do not forget the author of these ills'; the other Volumnius, to whom Plutarch owed his account of Brutus's end, failed to remember. He then recited the names of his comrades who had died in his defence. One of the men took a helmet to the river to fetch some water. There was a noise in the opposite direction, and Volumnius went to investigate. On returning he found that the water had been drunk up, and Brutus, 'with a very expressive smile', promised that more would be fetched for him. The man was sent to the river again, but was wounded by the enemy and escaped only with difficulty. Then one of the men decided to make his way to the camp to see if it was still intact; he succeeded in getting there safely and making the prearranged signal, but met the enemy on the way back and was killed.

Time passed. Brutus said something to his servant Clitus and then to his shield bearer Dardanus. Finally he asked Volumnius if he would hold his sword and help him to put an end to his life. Volumnius refused, as did the others, but when one of them said they should escape Brutus said, 'Yes indeed, we must escape, but with our hands not with our feet.'

Then, looking quite cheerful, he shook hands with each of them, saying that he was exceeding glad that none of his friends had been false to him. For his country's sake he blamed fortune; so far as he was concerned, he considered himself more blessed than the victors, not only yesterday and the day before, but now too, since he was leaving behind a reputation for virtue, which those who had gained power by arms or money would not do, nor could they prevent men thinking that the unjust and wicked who destroyed the just and good did not deserve to rule. Then after urgently beseeching them to save themselves he retired a certain distance in the company of two or three, including Strato, who had taught him rhetoric and remained a close friend. He placed Strato nearest himself and grasping his bare sword by the hilt with both hands he fell on it and died. There are however those who say that it was not he but Strato who, yielding to Brutus's insistence, held the sword with averted eyes while Brutus fell on it, with such force that it went through his breast and he died immediately.[25]

This is Plutarch's account of Brutus's end, and so far as it is based on Volumnius's memoir it should be reliable. It should certainly be preferred to that of Dio, according to which immediately before his suicide he quoted two lines which an unknown tragic poet put into the mouth of the dying Heracles: 'Wretched Virtue, so you were a mere word, whereas I followed you as a reality, and you were a slave to Fortune.'[26] This is inconsistent with Plutarch's account. Some have tried to reconcile the two by supposing that the address to Virtue was the quotation which Volumnius forgot, but in Plutarch's story this was uttered well before Brutus's final farewell to his friends, and apart from the fact that Plutarch speaks of two single lines whereas Dio makes Brutus quote a couplet, Volumnius is unlikely to have forgotten a much more memorable quotation than the one which he recorded; nor is it likely that if he forgot it and Plutarch did not know of it it would be known to Dio or his source. Moreover, the address to Virtue conflicts with Brutus's last words as given by Plutarch, which show him by no means disillusioned and still believing in virtue and in himself as a virtuous man. It conflicts too with all we know of Brutus and his conception of virtue as something independent of worldly success.

Although Dio's story was rejected as long ago as the sixteenth century by Victorius (Piero Vettori), it has been and still is accepted by reputable historians, and the idea that Brutus died disillusioned has become familiar. In the past these supposed last words were taken to illustrate the insufficiency of a virtue which was not supported by the Christian faith and the assurance it gave of a future life. To quote a widely read eighteenth-century historian,

'It is thus that virtue, which is purely human, and not founded upon the revelation of another life, where happiness will always reconcile itself to virtue, never fails to contradict itself.'[27] If we are right in rejecting Dio's story, this virtue did in fact sustain Brutus to the end.

Shakespeare ends his *Julius Caesar* with a fine tribute to Brutus by Antony, based on Plutarch, and a promise by Octavian to give him a worthy burial. What in fact happened to his body is uncertain. According to Plutarch Antony gave him an honourable funeral, and sent his ashes back to Servilia in Italy. Suetonius, however, states that Octavian sent his head to Rome to be cast down at the foot of Caesar's statue, and Dio adds that it never in fact reached Rome but was thrown overboard during a storm at sea, presumably because the sailors thought it was bringing them bad luck.[28] Whatever generous feelings Antony may have had, it is unlikely that Octavian would have shown any respect for the slayer of his adoptive father.

Brutus's career is full of anomalies and contradictions. The man of principle engaged in usurious money-lending. The hereditary enemy of Pompey fought on his side in the civil war. The friend and protegé of Caesar conspired against him and killed him. The student became a man of action, the lover of peace a commander in war. The champion of legality and constitutionalism assumed extraordinary powers in Macedonia and Asia Minor. The man who left Italy to avoid civil war made himself the leader of a great army against his fellow-countrymen. How are we to explain him?

Some have tried to deduce his character from his portraits. Boissier saw in one bust evidence of 'a narrow mind and an obstinate will . . . a strange sadness, that of a man overwhelmed by the weight of a great and fateful destiny', and in another, the head in the Capitoline Museum at Rome, he found that 'the sweetness and the sadness' remained while the 'sickly look' in the other bust had disappeared.[29] Unfortunately neither of these busts has much claim to be authentic. We have, however, some contemporary representations of him on his coins, and these are the nearest we can get to genuine portraits. To Gardthausen, author of a standard work on Augustus and his age, these suggested a gloomy philosopher rather than a statesman and man of action; the mouth had a sullen look, while the expression of the eye could be interpreted as denoting either energy or narrow-mindedness. To Professor Jocelyn Toynbee one of the coin portraits gives the impression of lack of self-confidence and weakness of character. Then there is a bust now in Madrid, which Professor Toynbee considers to have a good claim to represent Brutus; this shows a rather narrow face 'with a low brow, prominent cheek bones, a slightly negroid mouth, a projecting lower lip and a short chin-beard'.[30] If this is what Brutus really looked like he had not the advantage of a handsome face or an imposing presence. His features, if not ugly, might be called homely, and it is not easy to think of him as the bold and inspiring leader in the fight for freedom.

One may well imagine that, torn by the conflicting claims of friendship and principle, of natural inclinations and political or military necessity, he was a prey to doubts and inner conflict, was in Shakespeare's words a man 'with himself at war'. And yet that is hardly the impression given by other evidence. If there was that weakness and lack of self-confidence which Professor Toynbee sees in the coin portrait, it was well concealed. To all appearances Brutus was confident and sure of himself; *quicquid vult valde vult*, as Caesar said. His letters to Cicero and his utterances as recorded by Plutarch show him convinced of the justness of his cause and the rightness of his action. Irrespective of his interpretation of portrait busts, perhaps Boissier was on the right lines when he wrote: 'Slow and serious, he advanced step by step in everything, but once resolved, he was so absorbed in his conviction that nothing could divert him; he isolated and concentrated himself in it, he excited and inflamed himself for it by reflection and at last listened only to that inflexible logic that drove him to realize his purpose. He was one of those minds of which Saint-Simon says that they have an almost ferocious consistency. His obstinacy was the real source of his strength.'[31] If this characterization is sound we should think of Brutus not as a sensitive man but as one inclined to insensitivity.

There was something a little forbidding about him. Once when Atticus had given some advice which he thought unworthy Cicero asked him whether he was not deterred by the thought of the expression on Brutus's face.[32] Clearly he could look stern and disapproving. That he could be brusque and tactless, even rude, we have seen from his dealings with Cicero. On the other hand it is possible to make too much of this; he must have had a good deal of personal charm. Cicero once wrote of him: 'I have always loved Marcus Brutus for his fine intellect, the charm of his manners, and his outstanding uprightness and reliability.'[33] The letter which included these words was not perhaps one in which Cicero wrote with perfect frankness, but he would hardly have written of the charm of Brutus's manners (*suavissimos mores*) if he had always been as ungracious as he undoubtedly could be, on paper at any rate. According to Plutarch he was loved by his friends, and he uses the verb (ἐρᾶν) which is normally applied to the strongest and most passionate love.[34] Cicero said on several occasions that he loved Brutus (he had no inhibitions about using the words *amo* and *amor* in connection with friendship), and he was anxious, in vain it seems, for his feelings to be reciprocated. We are reminded of Dion, whom Plutarch aptly chose as the parallel to Brutus in Greek history. Dion, the former pupil in Plato's Academy, who persuaded his master to come to Sicily to educate Dionysius II of Syracuse and who eventually led an unsuccessful revolt against Dionysius, was like Brutus well-born, wealthy, cultured and high-minded. Like him, too, he was unaccommodating and lacking in tact; but at the same time he must have had some quality of charm which drew Plato to him and caused the strong personal attachment between the two men.

Elder men like Cicero and Atticus were attracted to Brutus. But he also had his circle of intimates of his own age, those friends who accompanied him on his campaigns, remained faithful to him, and were with him at the end. They were not well-born and influential Romans. Some of them were Greeks, others were intellectual Romans like the otherwise unknown Volumnius to whom we owe our knowledge of his last hours. Plutarch's admiring biography reflects the feelings of those who knew him best.

There was of course more to Brutus than personal charm. There were his abilities, which made him seem destined for a high place in Roman life; there was his character, which made him generally respected and admired. As for his abilities, it would be easy to depreciate them in view of his ultimate failure. He was perhaps too rigid to be a successful politician, and there is no evidence that he had any positive policy for the solution of Rome's troubles. But he was remembered as a model governor of Cisalpine Gaul, and after his initial inaction he showed unexpected qualities of vigour in organizing the Republican forces against the triumvirs. It was a considerable achievement to obtain control, as he did together with Cassius, of the Eastern Mediterranean and to build up the force which eventually met Octavian and Antony; and even if his generalship was faulty, he showed himself a courageous leader on the battle field. In an age in which public speaking was part of a politician's equipment he was an orator of note, though not in the highest class. He was scholarly and well read, and as a philosopher he shared with Cicero the distinction of providing Rome with a philosophical literature in Latin. He was no more of an original thinker than other Romans of his day, but his writings may well have been more independent of the Greeks than Cicero's. As we have seen, they left the reader with an impression of sincerity. Brutus was in fact endowed with a variety of talents, and there were not many Romans, even in that age of gifted all-rounders, who were equally distinguished in so many fields.

But it was his character rather than his talents that made him so highly respected. Cicero once wrote to Atticus: 'I shall never fail my friend Brutus, and this would be the case even if I had no personal connection with him, on account of his remarkable and extraordinarily fine character'; and in a letter to Brutus himself he expressed the hope that his son would be with him as much as possible because he could have no better training in character than by watching and imitating him.[35] On both occasions he used the word *virtus*. The English 'virtue' seems a little too stilted in the context of a letter, but something is lost by a paraphrase. *Virtus* suggests the manly vigour which one associates with the Romans, but it also suggests the moral ideal of the philosophers. As practised by Brutus it was essentially a philosophic concept; what he learnt from Aristus was what he tried to put into practice. This virtue gave a man the strength which came from a conviction that it was sufficient to itself and that all the supposed ills of life were of no account. It enabled him to face death with equanimity and even, though this may not have been authorized by the philosophers of the Academy, to take one's own life. Cato, as Cicero said, had shown the strength of virtue. Brutus too, like his uncle, proved its strength by seeking freedom through death. One can well believe that Caesar never really understood him. He was admitting his lack of understanding when he said, 'It's a great question what he wants, but whatever it is he wants he really does want it.' He could feel Brutus's earnestness and sincerity, but what inspired it was beyond his comprehension.

Today too the virtue which Brutus followed may not be easily understood, or if understood intellectually may not command much sympathy. It is the virtue of a pagan philosopher, not of a Christian saint, or of a modern humanitarian. 'In the insensibility of conscience, in the ignorance of the very idea of sin, in the contemplation of his own moral consistency, in the simple absence of fear, in the cloudless self-confidence, in the serene self-possession, in the cold self-satisfaction, we recognize the Philosopher.' So Cardinal Newman wrote of the deathbed scene of the Emperor Julian.[36] His words might well be applied to Brutus, and those who do not share Newman's faith would probably endorse some of his implied criticism. Nor is it easy for those who associate the fight for freedom with the rising of an oppressed populace to understand a champion of freedom who was an aristocrat of conservative temperament fighting to restore the status quo. For Brutus freedom meant having no one as master; specifically it meant open government, senatorial debates and annual magistracies, the old institutions of Rome which ensured that no one should have too much power. His belief in freedom derived from the traditions of Rome and of his family. It was an ideal which would appeal most strongly to those like himself, members of the governing class who could expect to hold the offices of state. It would not mean so much to the common people of Rome, or to those whom the Romans governed, or misgoverned, in the provinces. According to Dio the peoples of Greece who supported Brutus thought that he was going to bring them freedom.[37] If they expected to be relieved of Roman rule they would soon have been disabused had the battle of Philippi gone the other way. Nor did the Thapsians find that Brutus brought them freedom. Certainly freedom as understood by Brutus and the Republican politicians was limited and imperfect. When Augustus claimed that he had brought freedom to a people oppressed by a ruling clique[38] the claim, cynical though it may seem, had just enough truth in it to be plausible.

One of the mischances that afflicted the Republicans at Philippi was, if we can believe Plutarch, a delay in conveying to Brutus the news of a naval engagement in which his fleet had destroyed some reinforcements that were being brought to the Caesarians. If he had known of this in time, he would not have committed his forces in the second battle. But, says Plutarch, since Rome needed a monarchy, God willed that the one man who stood in the way of it should be removed.[39] Reading the story of Philippi and seeing how everything went wrong for the Republicans, one is tempted to agree with Plutarch and to feel that God, or Fate, was against Brutus, and that it was better that he should fail. Better if not for Rome at least for Brutus. For it is hard to believe that he would have made a success of liberating his country. He would not have abused his position if victorious, but more was needed than to remove the new tyrants and to let the old machinery of government get moving again. And nothing in Brutus's career suggests that he could have done, or would have wished to do, anything more than this.

This does not mean that there was nothing worth fighting for at Philippi. It may have been too late to save the Republic. The Republic may have needed reform as much as restoration. An efficient despotism like that of Augustus may bring greater benefits to the ordinary citizen than an inefficient republican regime. But public life is bound to suffer in the end when open discussion of political issues gives place to timid servility, when, as Tacitus puts it, men are ignorant of what goes on because they feel that politics does not belong to them.[40] Something was lost when the Roman Republic died on the field of Philippi. Messala, probably the ablest of the young Romans recruited by Brutus in Athens, played a leading part at Philippi, but after the defeat reconciled himself to Octavian and was later to be found fighting for him against Antony at Actium. When Octavian commented on the apparent inconsistency, Messala said that on both occasions he had been fighting for the better and juster cause.[41]

The cause of Brutus was better not only because it was that of freedom; it was also the cause of virtue. Horace, who like Messala reconciled himself to the new regime, wrote an ode addressed to an old friend and fellow soldier in Brutus's army, an otherwise unknown Pompeius. He recalled their companionship before Philippi and the battle itself, *cum fracta virtus*.[42] *Virtus* here is more than 'valour'. It recalls Brutus, who had written a book on virtue and had guided his life by it. Whatever Brutus's faults and inadequacies he had a moral elevation that no other Roman leader at the time had. Virtue was shattered at Philippi. But life went on, as it does after any disaster, and Horace had to find for himself a philosophy of life less heroic than that of Brutus and more suited to the new society.

CHAPTER TWO

THE REPUTATION OF A TYRANNICIDE

I FROM THE ROMAN EMPIRE TO THE RENAISSANCE

The murder of Caesar was the subject of controversy from the beginning. One influential voice, that of Cicero, welcomed it wholeheartedly. For him it was a glorious deed and its perpetrators were heroes, men of superhuman virtue. In the Second Philippic he observed that this was the first occasion in Roman history when a man had been killed who was not aiming at kingly power but actually exercising it. 'The deed is not only glorious and godlike in itself but also provides a clear example for imitation, especially as they have won a glory which the heavens can scarce contain. For even though there is sufficient reward in the mere consciousness of a noble deed, yet in my opinion immortality is not to be despised by a mortal.' It was not only in published works that he expressed opinions like this. He said much the same in a letter to Atticus. 'Everlasting glory will attend those heroes of ours, or should I rather say gods? Unpopularity there will be, and indeed danger, for them, but they have a great consolation in the consciousness of a fine and noble deed.'[1] And writing as a moral philosopher in *De Officiis*, which was completed after the Ides of March, he maintained that a tyrant had abrogated all claim to be regarded as a human being; he was a wild beast in the form of a man and should be removed from the body politic as a diseased limb had to be cut away from a human body. Was it a crime, he asked with obvious reference to Caesar, to kill a tyrant though he might be one's friend, and answered his question by claiming that the Romans regarded this as the finest of all deeds.[2]

Not all of them did. There is a moving and dignified letter to Cicero from a friend of Caesar's, C. Matius, in which he claims the right to grieve for his dead friend in spite of what his critics said about putting country before personal feelings – 'as if they had proved that his death was beneficial to the state'. They were threatening him for daring to criticize their action. 'What unheard of arrogance, that some should glory in the crime, and others not be allowed even to grieve with impunity. Why even slaves have always been free to feel fear, joy, sorrow as they like and not at another's dictation. And this freedom is what the self-styled liberators are trying to wrest from us by intimidation. But they will have no success. No fears for my safety will make me false to the claims of duty and humanity.'[3]

After the establishment in power of Augustus it was not to be expected that voices would be heard commending the murder of one who was not only the emperor's adoptive father but also had been officially deified. On the other hand there was nothing like an official condemnation of the memory of the tyrannicides. Brutus's writings remained in circulation, as did memoirs by men who had been closely associated with him.[4] The historians of the Augustan age who handled the civil wars, Pollio, Messala and Livy, were objective in their treatment and able to recognize the virtues of the Republican leaders.[5] Augustus himself could afford to be tolerant. Messala, as we have seen, could tell him that he had been on the better and juster side when fighting with Brutus. Another story tells how when passing through Milan Augustus accused the city authorities of harbouring an enemy of his. They were mystified, until he pointed to the statue of Brutus which still stood in the city. They were embarrassed at this and remained silent, until he smiled and praised them for not deserting their friends in adversity, and gave orders that the statue should stay where it was.[6]

Under Tiberius the atmosphere was less tolerant. In the year 22, when Cassius's widow, Brutus's half-sister, died at a great age, among the effigies of her family carried in the funeral procession Brutus and Cassius were conspicuous by their absence. Three years later the historian Cremutius Cordus was put on trial for having praised Brutus and described Cassius as the last of the Romans. He made, if we can believe Tacitus, an effective speech in his own defence, but he had already decided to put an end to his life, and after he had done so the Senate decreed that his books should be burnt.[7] Under Nero admiration for Brutus could be interpreted as treasonable, as when Thrasea's accuser described him as one who tried to emulate Brutus.[8] Not much credence however should be given to what was said to discredit one who incurred the emperor's displeasure; Thrasea's model seems to have been Cato rather than Brutus, and admiration for Cato was only to be expected in a Stoic. If, as Juvenal says, Thrasea used to celebrate the birthdays of Brutus and Cassius, this certainly looks like a political gesture. On the other hand the statues of Brutus, Cassius and Cato which adorned the house of Pliny's friend Titinius Capito do not seem to have implied any protest against the imperial system; indeed Capito, though Pliny does not mention the fact, was in the imperial service under Domitian, Nerva and Trajan successively.[9]

Those who know how efficiently modern states can form opinion and suppress dissident views might be inclined to think that under the Empire no one would venture to say a good word for the champion of Republican freedom. This would be far from the truth. It was possible to admire Brutus without approving his killing of Caesar. He could be recognized as a virtuous man who had yet done something which could only be deplored. To take the deed first, this, with one exception to which we shall come shortly, was condemned. The imperial historians Velleius Paterculus, Appian and Dio Cassius all express their disapproval and Valerius Maximus outdoes them all in his expressions of abhorrence. Even Plutarch, in general so favourable to Brutus, allows that monarchical rule was a necessary development, and pertinently questions whether so mild an autocrat as Caesar could really be counted as a tyrant.[10] Seneca's treatment of the question is interesting, because he does not simply condemn; he gives a reasoned criticism of Brutus's action. He would naturally be well disposed to a philosopher and one whose position was close to that of the Stoics; in one place he describes him as worthy of even Cato's admiration, which is high praise from a Stoic of the Roman Empire. He regards him as mistaken in his action rather than criminal. One mistake was to be frightened of the name of king, when according to the Stoics the best form of state was that ruled by a just king. Another was to hope for freedom when the rewards of power, and of subservience to power, were so great. He was wrong too in thinking that the old constitution could be restored when the old moral standards were lost, or that the rule of law could be established when he had seen so many men fighting to decide not whether they would be slaves but which master they would serve. Finally, he must have forgotten the lesson both of human nature and of history if he thought that after Caesar's death others would not appear with the same aims as his.[11]

Another, and rather different, issue was that of Brutus's obligation to Caesar. A question often discussed, according to Seneca, was whether he should have accepted life at Caesar's hands if he thought he deserved to be killed. Here Seneca defends Brutus. His action he considers to have been perfectly justifiable; he was under no obligation, because it was by wrongdoing that Caesar had acquired the power to confer a benefit. Caesar refrained from killing Brutus, but this was not the same thing as preserving his life.[12] Plutarch takes a different line. He admits that the gravest charge against Brutus is that he killed the man who had preserved him and treated him as friend. He points out, however, that this could be counted to his credit; he had no personal grievance against Caesar, but was inspired by a disinterested hatred of tyranny. Devotion to the common good made him an enemy of Caesar as it had made him a friend of Pompey.[13]

The cool, indeed critical, attitude of Seneca to Julius Caesar develops in his nephew into one of pronounced and prejudiced hostility. Lucan makes him the villain of his epic, and openly approves his assassination. He was himself potentially another Brutus. Like Brutus he plotted to kill one whom he regarded as a tyrant, and the intended victim, Nero, had been, as Caesar had been to Brutus, his friend and benefactor. Like Brutus too he was something of a philosopher, though he lacked Brutus's *gravitas* and moral elevation. He must indeed have been more of a liability than an asset to the Pisonian conspiracy, with his threats and his boasts, and his open glorification of tyrannicide, not to mention his weakness when his complicity was discovered.[14]

His epic poem on the Civil War breaks off abruptly in the course of Caesar's operations in Alexandria, and was evidently incomplete at his death. It is likely that if he had lived to finish it he would have taken the story as far as the Ides of March, in which case Brutus would have been a prominent figure in the final stages and along with Pompey and Cato one of Lucan's heroes. (On Pompey's death, according to Lucan, his spirit passed to Cato and Brutus.[15]) Though Brutus played a very minor role in the events covered by the existing books there are several passages which look forward to his future importance. In one of the early books he seeks the advice of Cato on whether to join in the war, and is given a long speech which ends with the claim that he will be fighting for freedom and law and therefore, though he is now the enemy of neither Pompey nor Caesar, he will be the enemy of whichever is the victor.[16] At the battle of Pharsalus Lucan makes Brutus disguise himself as a common soldier and attempt to kill Caesar. The incident was invented so that he could apostrophize Brutus and urge him not to anticipate the glorious deed he was to perform later.

O glory of Rome, last hope of the Senate, latest bearer of a name renowned throughout the ages, rush not too rashly through the midst of the enemy, and do not bring Philippi on yourself before the fated time. Death will come to you at your own Pharsalia. There is no point in aiming at Caesar's throat here. He has not yet occupied the citadel of power; he has yet to pass beyond the bounds of law, above the height which overtops all things, and to earn from fate so glorious a death. Let him live to be king, so that he may fall the victim of Brutus.[17]

There is yet another pointer to the future in the final book, when Pothinus, who had murdered Pompey on his arrival in Egypt, plots to do the same to Caesar. Lucan appeals to the fates not to allow Caesar to fall by any other hand than that of Brutus. If he were to be killed by Pothinus, it would simply add to the guilt of Egypt, and the warning to tyrants which Brutus was to give would be lost.[18]

We do not go to Lucan for subtle character drawing. His Brutus is a lay figure, a symbol, champion of liberty and warning to tyrants. It is as if only one side of that coin of his was visible. We see the daggers, the cap of liberty, and the inscription 'Ides of March', but the face of Brutus is invisible.

Lucan was unique among the writers of the Empire in his commendation of Caesar's murder. But even those who deplored the act could yet admire Brutus as a man of high principles. Velleius and Valerius Maximus acknowledge his virtues even though they consider them to have been outweighed by the crime of assassination, and Velleius emphasizes his moral superiority in his epigrammatic comparison of the two Republican leaders. 'Cassius was the better general as Brutus was the better man. Of the two one would prefer to have Brutus as friend, but one would fear Cassius more as enemy. In one there was more vigour, in the other more virtue. As it was better for Rome to have Caesar as leader than Antony, so, if they had been victorious, it would have been better to have Brutus than Cassius.'[19] Plutarch paints the picture of a fine character, gentle, magnanimous, free from anger, greed and desire for pleasure, upright and unbending in his championship of the right and the good, one whose high principles and lack of self-interest contrasted with the less pure motives of Cassius.[20] Finally, for Juvenal Brutus and his uncle Cato are types of the good man as Catiline is of the bad.

> *Catilinam*
> *quocunque in populo videas, quocunque sub axe,*
> *sed nec Brutus erit Bruti nec avunculus usquam.*[21]

Hence Catilines in every clime abound,
But where are Cato and his nephew found!

(Gifford's translation)

Before we leave the ancient world mention should be made of a brief but interesting reference to Brutus in the first book of the Meditations of Marcus Aurelius, where he pays a tribute to his teachers and others to whom he has reason to feel gratitude. Among them is Claudius Severus, a philosophically minded Roman, through whom, he says, he got to understand Thrasea, Helvidius Priscus, Cato, Dion and Brutus, and he goes on to say that he learnt from Severus 'to conceive the idea of a commonwealth based on equity and freedom of speech, and of a monarchy cherishing above all the liberty of the subject'.[22] The men whom Severus taught him to understand had all been inspired by philosophy and opposed to despotism; they had been in various ways failures and had either been put to death or taken their own lives. They and their ideals are now accepted by the emperor himself. Brutus is not now a symbol of opposition to the imperial power; he is looked up to as one from whom that power can learn something.

In the last and lowest circle of Dante's Inferno is Satan himself, with three heads, and from each of them hangs a figure undergoing punishment. The three sinners are Judas Iscariot, Brutus and Cassius, the men who betrayed their lords and benefactors.[23] That Dante should have placed the slayers of Caesar in the depths of hell is not surprising in view of the admiration he felt for the Roman Empire. And yet in *De Monarchia*, where he argued that the Empire was in accordance with the will of God and that its power was exercised for the general good, he also wrote in praise of Cato who 'showed the value of liberty when he preferred to leave this life a free man rather than remain in it deprived of freedom'.[24] And at the beginning of *Purgatorio* Dante with his guide Virgil comes across the venerable figure of Cato who, as Virgil informs him, knew how precious freedom was because he gave his life for it. Cato and Brutus were both champions of freedom and both were enemies of Caesar, yet Dante regards them very differently. In part this can be explained by the authority of Virgil, who had included in his description of the shield of Aeneas a scene in the world below where Cato was to be seen among the good dispensing justice.[25] But there is no consistent political doctrine behind Dante's picture of the ancient world. Cato is chosen as an example of devotion to freedom, Brutus as an example of treachery. It was of no concern to Dante that the two men were inspired by the same cause.

Dante's conception of Brutus as simply the betrayer of his friend is found also in Chaucer, in his brief reference to 'this false Brutus' in the Monk's Tale.[26] It is found too in writers of the Renaissance period. Sir Thomas Elyott in his *Governour* (1531) wrote:

Disloyalte or treason seldome escapeth great vengeance, all be it that it be pretended for a necessary purpose. Example we have of Brutus and Cassius, two noble Romaynes, and men of excellent virtues, which pretendynge an honorable zeale to the liberte and commune weale of their citie, slewe Julius Cesar (who trusted them most of all other) for that he usurped to have the perpetuall dominion of the empire, supposinge thereby to have brought the Senate and people to their pristinate liberte. But it did not so succede to their purpose.

Similarly John Carion, whose Chronicle appeared in 1532, roundly condemned the assassination of Caesar and pointed out that 'God suffred so greate a mischievousnesse not longe unpunished. For as manye as had conspired to the death of Julius, were also slayne themselves not long after.' And when in 1578 an English translation of Appian appeared, its dedication included the words, 'How God plagueth them that conspire againste theyr Prince, this Historie declareth at the full.'²⁷

Meanwhile, beginning with John of Salisbury in the mid-twelfth century, the question of the limits of obedience and the right to resist authority had been the subject of discussion from a theoretical point of view. This discussion was based on the classical tradition of political thought, with its distinction between the good king, subject to law and ruling in the interests of his people, and the tyrant, free from all restraints, whose rule was the worst of all types of government. And one of the most accessible of ancient writings, Cicero's *De Officiis*, not only provided a theoretical justification of tyrannicide, but did so with particular reference to the assassination of Caesar. John of Salisbury, who was well versed in classical literature, defends tyrannicide as not only lawful but also just and right. In his view the tyrant is the image of satanic wickedness as the good king, whom he calls *princeps*, is of divinity. He has some doubts however about Julius Caesar, pointing out that no tyrant was nearer than he to a *princeps*, and that all his acts had been approved by the Roman people, though as he had gained control of the state by armed force he was held to be a tyrant. He is no less fair to Brutus, whom he sees as animated by love of liberty, than which nothing could be more desirable.²⁸

Thomas Aquinas did not go quite as far as John of Salisbury in approving tyrannicide. He discussed the question in two works, one early and the other late. In the first he concluded that a Christian was not obliged to obey a tyrant if power had been acquired by violence or illegally; he referred to Cicero's justification of Caesar's assassination in *De Officiis* and mentioned with apparent approval the praise accorded those who killed tyrants in order to liberate their country.²⁹ In the later work, which was published posthumously, he gives the matter more thorough consideration and is more cautious in his conclusions. He adopts the Aristotelian distinction between the just and the unjust types of rule, with tyranny as the worst of the latter. But he does not go so far as to allow tyrannicide. He observes that if the tyranny is a mild one action against the tyrant may only result in a worse state of affairs. Even if the tyranny becomes unbearable, to kill the tyrant is not in accordance with apostolic teaching. If the people has the right to appoint the king it may also depose him or limit his powers, and if he is appointed by a higher authority appeal may be made to that authority; but if no such aid can be got from man there is nothing left but to resort to God.[30]

The debate went on. To classical arguments and classical precedents was added the testimony of the Bible. This, however, was far from clear. On the one hand the Old Testament provided examples of rulers who had been slain with the apparent approval of the Almighty, such as Eglon, in whose fat Ehud thrust his dagger, and Jehoram, treacherously shot by Jehu.[31] On the other hand St Paul had laid down that the powers that be are ordained of God, and the early Christians had been quite content to put up with Roman emperors who could well be called tyrants. It was not Christians who conspired to kill Domitian. The Reformation gave a new actuality to the question. For the Protestant under a Catholic ruler or the Catholic under a Protestant one there was a religious motive for resistance, and one likely to be stronger than classical precedent or rational calculation of advantages. The experience of French Protestants under persecution led to the writing of a number of works on the right to resist the oppressor, notably the anonymous *Vindiciae contra Tyrannos*, published in 1579. And in Scotland, where a Catholic queen had been deposed, George Buchanan published, also in 1579, his *De Jure Regni apud Scotos* in which he argued for the right of the people to take action against a ruler who had misused his, or her, power. On the Catholic side tyrannicide found a defender in the Spanish Jesuit Juan de Mariana. In 1589 a Dominican monk, after consulting the theologians of his order, murdered Henry III of France, because he had designated the Protestant Henry of Navarre as his heir, and Mariana specifically approved this action in his treatise *De Rege et Regis Institutione*.[32]

In spite of his classical learning and his use of classical political ideas, Buchanan did not mention the case of Caesar, and Mariana referred to it only incidentally. The author of the *Vindiciae* provocatively recalled Roman Republicanism in the pseudonym under which he wrote – Junius Brutus. His text is less provocative. He approved the assassination of Caesar, but with qualifications. He observed that Caesar's tyranny was only in its early stages, when it was legitimate to try to check it by assassination. When a tyranny was firmly established and the tyrant had obtained some sort of formal consent to his rule, the only thing to do was to put up with it.[33]

In Italy of the Renaissance men felt nearer to classical Rome than they did elsewhere, and Brutus was more of a living figure. The tradition of ancient Republicanism was alive even in the fourteenth century, when Rienzi had himself elected tribune in Rome and was described by Petrarch as the third Brutus, and when Boccaccio could declare that there was scarcely any sacrifice more acceptable to God than the blood of a tyrant.[34] Brutus was however a controversial figure for a reason peculiar to Italy, his treatment by Dante. Humanist scholars who had learnt from antiquity of the wickedness of tyrants and the virtues of their slayers, Brutus in particular, had to take into account the views of Italy's great poet. One of them, Coluccio Salutati, came down on the side of Dante. In his *De Tyranno* (1400) he paid particular attention to the assassination of Caesar. He argued that Caesar could not reasonably be called a tyrant and therefore his murder was not justified. 'Who would not say that his assassins were wrong rather than right in laying their criminal hands on the father of their country, the man who with every right was ruler of the world?' The principal conspirators had held office under Caesar and his acts had been ratified by the Senate; nor was Cicero right in claiming that the murder had the approval of all good men. Moreover, government by a good king was the best form of constitution, and Rome at that time needed a monarchy. Salutati concludes that Dante was right in consigning Brutus and Cassius to the bottommost hell.[35] In another work he uses the fate of Brutus and Cassius to illustrate the thesis that apparently fortuitous events are part of the divine design. It might appear to be an accident that deprived Brutus of victory at Philippi, but none the less Providence had ordained that Octavian should have the victory so that he could establish the united and peaceful world into which Christ was born.[36]

Others tried to reconcile Dante with the admiration which they thought should belong to tyrannicides by supposing that Brutus and Cassius in the *Inferno* were symbols rather than historical characters. This view, which has some truth in it, was put forward by Leonardo Bruni in a dialogue which purports to reproduce a conversation between Salutati and others including Niccolo Niccoli, an enthusiastic admirer of antiquity, born like Bruni himself a generation later than Salutati.

Are we to believe [asks Niccoli] that Dante, the most learned man of his age, did not know in what manner Caesar achieved dominion – that he did not know of the rape of liberty, the abject fear of the people when Marc Antony placed the crown on Caesar's head? Do you believe he did not know what *virtus* Brutus possessed in the judgment of all historical tradition? . . . Dante knew it well, he knew it precisely, but he presented to us, in the image of Caesar, the legitimate prince and most just monarch of the world and, in the image of Brutus, the rebellious troublesome villain who criminally murdered this prince. Not because Brutus was such a man; had he been such a one, how could he have been praised by the Senate as the restorer of liberty? But the poet took this material as the subject of his poem because Caesar, in whatever manner, had wielded royal power and because Brutus, together with more than sixty of the noblest citizens, had slain him.[37]

The same idea was adopted by Cristoforo Landino in his commentary on Dante of 1481. The Roman emperor, he argues, was head of the temporal government of Christendom as the Pope was of the spiritual; therefore Dante took Caesar as representing the empire and did not mean the historical Caesar, who was a usurper, while Brutus and Cassius were not themselves but represented destroyers of the true monarch, just as Cato in *Purgatorio* represented liberty. 'It would certainly have been unheard of cruelty and wholly alien to the learning and equity of so great a poet to inflict eternal punishment, and a punishment so severe, on those whose fervent devotion led them to death in the hope of freeing their country from the yoke of servitude by a deed which had they been Christians would have won them a place of honour in the highest heaven.' He does not deny that Caesar was a great and gifted man, but none the less his aim was to deprive his country of liberty by force and it was for that reason that he was killed. 'A study of the

laws of any well constituted republic will show that to no one is
offered a greater reward than to the man who kills a tyrant.'³⁸

Landino like Bruni and Niccoli was a Florentine, and in Florence
with its tradition of republican government the spirit of freedom,
nourished by the revival of learning, was particularly strong.
Admiration of Brutus was not merely academic. When Lorenzino
de' Medici murdered his cousin the Duke Alessandro in 1537 he
considered himself and was considered by others as a second Brutus,
a liberator and tyrannicide.³⁹ He was hailed as the Tuscan Brutus
and praised in Latin verse as having done single-handed what
Brutus had done along with many fellow conspirators. He struck
a medal in obvious imitation of the famous coin of Brutus, with his
portrait on one side and on the other the cap of liberty between two
daggers, with the inscription VIII ID IAN. His exploit needed some
adventitious justification. He was little better than his worthless
cousin, and the assassination was a brutal affair. Nor did it achieve
anything. It only resulted in the accession of a new Medici Duke,
an Augustus, as was observed at the time, in place of a Caesar.

The incident is of interest not only as an illustration of the cult of
tyrannicide and the influence of ancient republicanism but also
because it gave rise indirectly to a notable work of art, Michelangelo's bust of Brutus now in the Bargello at Florence. Donato
Giannotti, a former Secretary of State at Florence, left the city for
Rome in 1539 to enter the service of Cardinal Ridolfi, who had
unsuccessfully tried to restore the Florentine Republic after the
death of Alessandro. Giannotti was an upholder of republicanism
and an admirer of Brutus, and it was he who persuaded Michelangelo to execute the bust for Ridolfi. Michelangelo created a
Brutus not as he appears in the portraits on his coins but rather as
one might imagine a heroic tyrannicide, handsome, self-confident,
and aggressive. He left the work unfinished and it was said that this
was because of its political implications. An unfinished work of
Michelangelo requires no such explanation, but it may none the
less be that he had some doubts about the virtue of Brutus and of
tyrannicide. Giannotti wrote a dialogue between himself and
Michelangelo on Dante's treatment of Brutus which, if it is based
on actual conversations, shows that the sculptor was by no means
certain that Caesar had been justly slain.

Giannotti maintains that Brutus and Cassius should have been in a place of honour in paradise rather than at the bottom of hell. Dante must have been unaware that Caesar was a tyrant, or else he did not know that tyrannicides are universally praised and rewarded. Michelangelo answers that Dante must have known what a tyrant was; he points to the place that Cato the champion of freedom has in Purgatory and claims that Dante really believed Brutus and Cassius to have been justified in their act in that they killed one whom every citizen was bound to kill, one who was not a man but a beast in human form. He reconciles this view with Dante's apparent condemnation of the two conspirators by borrowing from Landino's exegesis and claiming that Dante's Caesar was not the historical Caesar and his slayers not the historical Brutus and Cassius; since Dante believed the Roman Empire to have been ordained by God it followed that whoever betrayed its founder betrayed the majesty of the Empire and consequently was to be punished as a betrayer of the divine majesty. Giannotti is not satisfied with this and Michelangelo now changes his ground and brings forward a number of pragmatic arguments against Brutus and Cassius. Did not their action, he asks, only lead to a worse situation, and would it not have been better to let Caesar live even if he did make himself king? If he had not been killed he might have restored liberty to Rome; he might have followed the example of Sulla and abdicated. It is an act of great presumption to kill any head of state whether just or unjust, and to commit a crime like murder is not the way to bring about good.[40] The discussion has moved away from Dante, and the murder of Caesar is now condemned irrespective of the poet's treatment of Brutus and Cassius. Michelangelo has the last word, and we are left with the impression that Giannotti was not so sure as he had been about the rightness of Brutus's action.

2 THE AGE OF REASON

It was the opinion of Thomas Hobbes that rebellion against monarchs was encouraged by the study of the classical authors. 'From the reading of such books,' he wrote in his *Leviathan*, 'men have undertaken to kill their Kings, because the Greek and Latin writers, in their books and discourses of Policy, make it lawfull and laudable, for any man to do so; provided before he do it he call him a tyrant.' And elsewhere in the same work he claimed that as a result of reading the classical authors 'men from their childhood have gotten a habit (under a false show of Liberty) of favouring tumults, and of licentious controlling the actions of their Sovereigns; and again of controlling those controllers, with the effusion of so much blood; as I think I may truly say, there was never any thing so deerly bought, as these Western parts have bought the learning of the Greek and Latine tongues.'[1]

The *Leviathan* appeared shortly after the English had got rid of their king, not by the crude method of assassination, but after what purported to be a legal trial. If Hobbes thought this action was to be attributed to influences from Greece and Rome he was probably mistaken. Admittedly Charles I was accused of being a tyrant and the word in itself recalls the ancient world; but it does not appear that classical thought and classical precedent had much influence on those who rebelled against him and had him executed. They believed that they were doing the Lord's work, and their apologists were more likely to quote the fate of Eglon than that of Caesar. The most distinguished of these apologists, John Milton, was unusually well versed in the classics, but in his *Tenure of Kings and Magistrates*, written immediately after Charles I's execution and designed to prove that 'it is lawful . . . to call to account a tyrant, or wicked king, and after due conviction, to depose, and put him to death', he alludes only briefly to the Greeks and Romans, 'lest it be objected they were Heathen'. As for the murder of Caesar, in spite of his Republican sympathies he could not give it unqualified approval. In his first Defence against Salmasius he observed that Caesar was killed as a tyrant, that his assassins were the most excellent men of his age, and that the deed had been highly praised by Cicero; but 'I could have wished that he if any tyrant could have been spared'. And in his Commonplace Book he wrote of 'the error of the noble Brutus and Cassius who felt themselves of spirit to free a nation, but consider'd not that the nation was not fit to be free'.[2]

Although in general classical republicanism had little influence on the English Parliamentarians this does not apply to one of them,

Algernon Sidney. He was considered to have modelled himself on Brutus, and James Thomson, in his *Seasons*, called him 'the British Brutus' (or 'Cassius' in later editions),

> Of high determin'd spirit, roughly brave,
> By ancient learning to the enlighten'd love
> Of ancient freedom warmed.[3]

In his *Discourses concerning Government* Sidney wrote of Julius Caesar as one of those who usurped power by force or fraud and of Brutus and Cassius's 'noble attempt' to restore their country's liberty, and when he was living in retirement at his country house of Penshurst under the Protectorate he himself took the part of Brutus in a private production of Shakespeare's *Julius Caesar*. He had indeed a certain resemblance to Brutus. Like him he was of aristocratic birth, a man of principle, somewhat rigid and doctrinaire in his republicanism. When he was in Denmark on a diplomatic mission he wrote in the album of the University of Copenhagen the words *manus haec inimica tyrannis*, and defending himself to his father for the use of these words he avowed himself an enemy to tyrants 'having never heard, that any sort of men were so worthily the objects of enmity'. He did not, however, emulate Brutus's tyrannicide. The hand that was so hostile to tyrants was not raised against Charles I. Sidney believed in the right of the people to remove their kings, but he strongly objected to the illegality of Charles's trial and he protested against it. He was moreover as much opposed to the despotism of Cromwell as to that of the King. When Cromwell dissolved Parliament he retired from politics, and when he acted the part of Brutus at Penshurst some of his lines were taken as a reflection on Cromwell.[4]

As this incident shows, Brutus remained the exemplar of the tyrannicide, and in times of political tension and suspicion he could take on a contemporary significance. Here it seems lies the explanation of the Pindarick Ode by Abraham Cowley published in 1656 in which he addressed Brutus in terms of extravagant admiration,

> Excellent Brutus, of all humane race
> The best till *Nature* was improv'd by *Grace*

and went on to defend his action in slaying Caesar.

From thy strict rule some think that thou didst swerve
(*Mistaken Honest men*) in *Caesars* blood;
What *Mercy* could the *Tyrants Life* deserve
From him who kill'd *Himself* rather than serve? . . .
　　Ingrateful Brutus do they call?
Ingrateful Caesar, who could *Rome* enthrall!
An act more barbarous and unnatural
(In th' exact ballance of true *Virtue* try'de)
Then his *Successor Nero's Parricide*!
　　There's none but *Brutus* could deserve
　　That all men else should *wish* to *serve*,
And *Caesars* usurpt place to him should proffer;
None can deserve 't but he who would *refuse* the offer.

In a later stanza he asks

What joy can *humane things* to us afford
When we see perish thus by odde events,
　　Ill men and wretched *Accidents*,
The *best Cause* and *best Man* that ever drew a *Sword*?
　　　　When we see
The false *Octavius* and wild *Antonie*,
　　God-like Brutus, conquer Thee?
What can we say but thine own *Tragick Word*,
That *Virtue*, which had worship't been by thee,
As the most solid *Good*, and greatest *Deitie*,
　　By this fatal proof became
　　An *Idol* only, and a *Name*.

But after apparently associating himself with Brutus's alleged last
words Cowley ends on a more orthodox note:

　　Hold noble Brutus and restrain
The bold voyce of thy generous *Disdain* . . .
A few years more, so soon hadst thou not dy'ed
Would have confounded *Humane Virtues* pride,
　　And shew'd thee a *God crucifi'ed*.

　Cowley had served the Stuarts in exile, but he reconciled himself
to the Commonwealth, and it looks very much as if under the
names of Brutus and Caesar he was attempting to prove his change
of allegiance by justifying the execution of Charles I, while the
lines about Brutus succeeding to Caesar's power seem designed to
fit Cromwell. The ode appears to have been taken by contem-

poraries as having a topical reference. It is said that after the Restoration Cowley petitioned for some reward for his services to the royal cause. The Lord Chancellor, Clarendon, 'turn'd on him, and with *a severe countenance*, said, *Mr Cowley, your Pardon is your Reward*, letting him know, the King's forgiving him that *Ode*, was more than he merited; that he could not be ignorant, there were Enthusiastical *Republicans* who, notwithstanding the Turn of Affairs, still retain'd as good an Opinion of their Cause, as ever Brutus cou'd have of his: And cou'd he expect that his Royal Master shou'd promote one, who, as far as his Poetic Vein cou'd carry him, had encourag'd these desperate Men, to make an attempt on his Sacred Person.'[5]

After the Glorious Revolution of 1688 there was little danger of Britain needing a Brutus to put an end to despotic rule. The monarchy was now sufficiently tamed. Though their country was ruled by a king the British liked to think of it as the home of freedom. This is the theme of several poets of the eighteenth century. They visited Rome and saw the sad state to which the city had fallen. They attributed its decline to the loss of freedom, and considered that their own country had taken the place of the free Rome of Republican times. James Dyer in his *Ruins of Rome*, addressing Liberty, adapts Virgil's famous lines on Rome's mission:

> But thou, thy nobler Britons teach to rule:
> To check the ravage of tyrannic sway;
> To quell the proud; to spread the joys of peace,
> And various blessings of ingenuous trade.
> Be these our arts; and ever may we guard,
> Ever defend thee with undaunted heart.

Lord Lyttleton, in a poetic epistle to Pope written in Rome, claimed that

> From tyrants, and from priests, the Muses fly,
> Daughters of Reason and of Liberty,

and that they had left Italy for 'Thames's flowery borders'. George Keate, also writing in Rome, asks of Liberty,

> found no more
> In these once favour'd seats, where shall our steps
> Pursue thy flight?

and answers 'To Britain'.[6] This theme is elaborated in James Thomson's *Liberty*. He calls up Liberty personified, 'her temples bound with British oak', and makes her warn Britain, whither she has migrated from Rome, never to allow herself to suffer the same fate as Rome. It was at Philippi that she had finally left Rome.

> To these vile wars I left ambitious slaves,
> And from Philippi's field, from where in dust
> The last of Romans, matchless Brutus! lay
> Spread to the north untamed a rapid wing.[7]

The somewhat complacent self-satisfaction expressed by writers like Thomson was tempered by a feeling that the British hardly lived up to the example set by the great heroes of Rome. It was generally accepted that the Romans were pre-eminent in virtue and that such virtue was rarely found in modern times. Swift once wrote that the good opinion he had expressed of the present ministry did not mean that they were men of 'sublime abstracted *Roman* virtue'.[8] Idealization of the Romans was encouraged by a thorough but uncritical classical education. Men could read in Livy of the heroes of early days and in Lucan of the virtues of Cato. They accepted what the Romans said about themselves, or rather about their predecessors, for the tendency always was to idealize the men of earlier ages and look back to the past for models to imitate.

The cult of antiquity and the cult of freedom were combined in Addison's *Cato*, which drew admiring crowds when performed in London in 1713. In the figure of Cato Roman virtue was displayed on the stage for all to see and admire. According to a contemporary versifier,

> Now first on Albion's theatre we see
> A perfect image of what man should be.[9]

With Cato it was natural to couple Brutus, as Juvenal had done. Musing on the heroes of antiquity, James Thomson mentions a number of names from Rome – Numa, Camillus, Fabricius, Cincinnatus, Regulus, Scipio and Cicero – ending with

> Unconquered Cato, virtuous in extreme;
> And thou, unhappy Brutus, kind of heart,

Whose steady arm, by awful virtue urg'd,
Lifted the Roman steel against thy friend.[10]

'Cato and Brutus,' wrote Swift in one of his political tracts, 'were the two most virtuous men in Rome.' And in *Gulliver's Travels* he brings Gulliver to an island where the Governor has at his disposal magicians who can call up the dead. At Gulliver's request Caesar and Brutus appear.

I was struck with a profound veneration at the sight of *Brutus*, and could easily discover the most consummate Virtue, the greatest Intrepidity, and Firmness of Mind, the truest Love of his Country, and general Benevolence for Mankind in every Lineament of his Countenance. I observed with much Pleasure that these two Persons were in good Intelligence with each other; and *Caesar* freely confessed to me, that the greatest Actions of his own Life were not equal by many Degrees to the Glory of taking it away. I had the Honour to have much Conversation with *Brutus*; and was told that his ancestor Junius, Socrates, Epaminondas, Cato the Younger, Sir Thomas More and himself, were perpetually together: A Sextumvirate to which all the Ages of the World cannot add a seventh.[11]

Swift found much in the contemporary world to arouse his disgust and indignation, and he expressed his feelings about the present by contrasting it with an idealized past. But it was not only dislike of his own age which made him present such a favourable picture of Brutus. He would not have engaged in or advocated assassination, but he was in his own way a champion of freedom and his love of freedom owed something to the classics. He once described himself in conversation as 'having been long conversant with the Greek and Latin authors, and therefore a lover of liberty', and in one of his Irish Tracts he admitted that he was 'justly liable to the Censure of *Hobbs*, who complains, that the youth of *England* imbibe ill opinions, from reading the Histories of ancient *Greece* and *Rome*, those renowned Scenes of Liberty and every Virtue'.[12]

A few years before the publication of *Gulliver's Travels* there appeared a series of papers with the title *Cato's Letters*, which had a wide circulation. The pseudonym Cato indicates the tendency of the work, as does the subtitle, 'Essays on Liberty, Civil and Religious'. One of the authors responsible, a Scotsman called

Thomas Gordon, who, as his translations of Tacitus and Sallust show, had some claims to classical scholarship, contributed some papers in praise of Brutus. Two of these consisted of translations of the two long letters Brutus wrote in criticism of Cicero; two others defend Brutus for his killing of Julius Caesar. Gordon is a fervent admirer of Brutus, whom he describes as 'perhaps the most amiable character, the most accomplished man, that ever the world saw'. The reasoning in his letter to Cicero, so Gordon claims, shows him 'to have been animated by a most sublime and glorious spirit of virtue and liberty, and is so stupendously strong, that his eloquence must have been as great as his soul'. As for Caesar, he was un-doubtedly a tyrant, and 'it is a known maxim of liberty among the great, the wise, the free ancients . . . that every man has a right to destroy one who would destroy all men'. Caesar was 'one of the greatest robbers and murderers that ever lived', a man consum-mately wicked; Brutus, 'who owned no allegiance but to the commonwealth, scorned the deceitful smiles and generosity of its oppressor'.[13] Gordon's rather naive effusions led to suspicions that he was a republican and an enemy to kings. This he denied, claim-ing that the king had no better subject than 'Cato'. The British sovereign was far from being a tyrant, and the arguments in favour of Brutus's tyrannicide did not concern 'our free and legal govern-ment' except in so far as they supplied arguments in its defence. The letters of Brutus which he translated were presumably unfamiliar to most of his readers, and there were those who thought that his name and that of Cicero concealed those of two contemporaries. To them Gordon replied that Brutus was Brutus and no one else and Cicero was Cicero.[14]

Brutus continued to be celebrated as the heroic champion of freedom. Lord Nugent's *Ode on Mr Pulteney* of 1739 included the lines

> Though CATO liv'd, though TULLY spoke,
> Though BRUTUS dealt the godlike stroke,
>   Yet perish'd fated Rome.[15]

And in 1765, in the second book of his *Pleasures of the Imagination*, Mark Akenside, who, according to Dr Johnson, retained from his Dissenting upbringing 'an unnecessary and outrageous zeal for what he called and thought liberty', asked, in what is said to have been the best remembered passage in his works,[16]

> Is there in the abyss,
> Is there, among the adamantine spheres
> Wheeling unshaken through the boundless void,
> Aught that with half such majesty can fill
> The human bosom, as when Brutus rose
> Refulgent from the stroke of Caesar's fate
> Amid the crowd of patriots; and, his arm
> Aloft extending like eternal Jove,
> When guilt brings down the thunder, call'd aloud
> On Tully's name, and shook the crimson sword
> Of justice, in his rapt astonish'd eye,
> And bade the father of his country hail,
> For lo, the tyrant prostrate on the dust
> And Rome again is free?

There were some who showed their devotion to republican freedom by wearing a signet ring based on the famous coin of Brutus with the daggers and the cap of liberty. Sylas Neville recorded in his diary in 1768 that he had acquired such a ring, which he intended to use 'when I write etc in my real character'; and in the next year he added a cane with a gold top engraved with the same emblems. The second Earl Harcourt, a friend of Rousseau and of various English writers and artists, also at one time wore a ring of this type. The practice, conspiratorial though it may seem, was harmless enough. Neville was an ineffective character whose professions of republicanism did not amount to much, and Lord Harcourt gave away his ring in 1784 as a sign that he had changed his views.[17]

Effusions such as that of Akenside were probably confined to Britain, where it was safe to profess an 'unnecessary and outrageous zeal' for liberty and possible to extol Brutus, as 'Cato' did, and still remain a loyal subject. For a continental view of Brutus we may turn to the article on him in Bayle's *Dictionnaire Historique et Critique*, first published in 1695–7. Here Brutus is described as an extreme republican, so infatuated by grand and noble ideas of liberty and patriotism that he was deterred neither by his obligations to Caesar nor by the certainty of advancement under him

from killing one whom he regarded as a tyrant. Bayle acknowledges Brutus's fine personal qualities, but regrets that they were
tarnished by the assassination of a benefactor. Disapproval of
Brutus's action did not however mean approval of Caesar. Far from
it. In Bayle's opinion Caesar deserved to die; but it was certainly
wrong for a few individuals to take upon themselves the function
of punishing him.[18] Whatever the disfavour with which Bayle was
regarded in his native France, his views on Brutus and Caesar would
have been acceptable under the Bourbon monarchy. Republicanism of course was not in favour, but neither was Caesarism. The
French monarchs were legitimate rulers, to be distinguished from
a usurper like Caesar. So we find J.-B. Crevier, who was responsible for the later volumes of Rollin's popular *Histoire Ancienne*,
acknowledging that Caesar deserved death while condemning
Brutus for taking the law into his own hands. In his view whoever
subverts the legitimate government, whether the rebellious subject
of a monarchy or, as in the case of Caesar, the usurper of power
under a Republic, deserves the severest punishment. But it does not
follow that everyone has a right to inflict this punishment. Brutus
punished a criminal, but as his action was unauthorized he should
be considered not the lawful avenger of the liberties of his country
but rather as no better than a homicide.[19] Crevier was not a man of
much note and it can be assumed that his views were those generally
accepted in the France of his day. They were correct but somewhat
academic. Montesquieu pertinently observed that the guilt of
Caesar consisted in placing himself out of reach of any punishment
but assassination.[20]

Before the eighteenth century ended the American colonies had
thrown off their allegiance to the crown and the ancient and
famous monarchy of France had ended in bloody revolution.
Hobbes might have seen in these revolutions an example of the
baleful influence of the Greek and Roman writers, for the ideals of
the revolutionaries were to a large extent drawn from the ancient
world. Religion was weaker than in the previous century; the
classical authors were widely read and the secular ideals of antiquity,
the spirit of liberty and heroic virtue, found a ready response at
least in those disposed to be dissatisfied with the regime under
which they lived. The influence of antiquity can be exaggerated;

Tom Paine may have been more influential than Plutarch. But, if
nothing more, Greece and Rome provided precedents and arguments which gave respectability to actions which had other motives than admiration for antiquity. As for Brutus, he was certainly
one of the heroes of the American revolutionaries. One might
think that there was little in common between the colonial situation and that of Rome in 44 BC and that George III was hardly
another Julius Caesar; but John Dickinson could say in 1754 that
Britain would soon be to America what Caesar was to Rome, and
Patrick Henry could claim that the king had degenerated into a
tyrant. We are told that Patrick Henry even went so far as to say
in a speech to the Virginia Assembly in 1765 that 'Tarquin and
Julius Caesar had their Brutus, Charles had his Cromwell, and he
did not doubt that some good American would stand up in favour
of his country'; and Josiah Quincy ended a pamphlet of 1774 with
an appeal to Americans to imitate that 'great and good man' Brutus
and like him dedicate themselves to the service of their country.[21]

In revolutionary France Brutus was for a time very much a name
to conjure with. There was a bust of Brutus near the orator's
tribune in the Convention, copies of which were reproduced in
porcelain and put on sale. A *fête de Brutus* was celebrated in the
cathedral of Nevers; and one provincial town found its patron St
Blaise replaced by Brutus. A section of Paris was named after
Brutus; there was a *Rue de Brutus*, and in the period when classical
forenames were in vogue his was one of the most popular. But
there were two famous Brutuses; and though some of the French-
men concerned may not have understood the difference, the one
thus honoured was, it appears, Lucius, the founder of the Roman
Republic, and not Marcus, who failed to restore it.[22] The classical
enthusiasm evinced by the name Brutus soon faded. The French
Republic was short-lived and it was not long before it gave place to
Empire. It had bred not new Brutuses but a new Caesar.

3 SOME MODERN VIEWS

With the development of historical studies in the eighteenth
century men began to look anew at the ancient world. The legen-
dary Brutus, the heroic champion of freedom, the embodiment of

Roman virtue, could not survive in the face of the profounder scholarship and more critical spirit now applied to the records of antiquity. In eighteenth-century England Nathaniel Hooke's *Roman History* (1738–71) was the standard work on the subject, and whatever its inadequacies it was at least an improvement on the superficial compilation of Lawrence Eachard (1695) which was the first comprehensive history of Rome in English. Hooke finds it impossible not to regret Caesar's death and charges his murderers with the basest ingratitude; he acknowledges Brutus's reputation in antiquity, but considers it 'greatly sullied by many instances of avarice, of pride and of cruelty'.[1] He appears to have been influenced by two writers from whom he quotes, both of whom had decided views on the subject. One was Colley Cibber, actor, playwright and poet laureate, author of a slight and superficial work on *The Character and Conduct of Cicero* (1747) which is marked by an extravagant admiration of Caesar of the sort we associate with the nineteenth rather than the eighteenth century. He sees Brutus as blinded by 'enthusiasm' and Caesar as the true champion of Rome's liberty, one who 'saved her from the worst of enemies herself', while Brutus saved her from an imaginary tyrant.[2] The other writer was a man whose views carried far more weight than those of Cibber, Conyers Middleton, whose *Life of Cicero* (1741) included a trenchant criticism of Brutus.

Middleton was no Caesar worshipper. His hero was Cicero, and those who study Cicero as he did are likely to side with him when he is criticized, as he was by Brutus. Middleton in fact conceived a strong dislike of Brutus. He draws up a comprehensive indictment of him which must have struck many of his readers as paradoxical.

In his outward manner and behaviour, he affected the rigor of a Stoic, and the severity of an old Roman; yet by a natural tenderness and compassion was oft betrayed into acts of effeminate weakness. To restore the liberty of his country, he killed his friend and benefactor . . . Yet he would not take Antony's life, though it was a necessary sacrifice to the same cause. When Dolabella had basely murdered Trebonius, and Antony openly approved the act, he could not be persuaded to make reprisals on C. Antony; but through a vain ostentation of clemency, suffered him to live, though with danger to himself. When his brother-in-law, Lepidus, was declared an enemy, he expressed an absurd and peevish resentment of it, for the sake of his nephews, as if it would not have been in his power to have repaired their fortunes, if the Republic was ever restored; or if not, in their father's. How contrary is this to the spirit of that old Brutus . . . He blames Cicero for dispensing honours too largely, yet claims an infinite share of them to himself; and, when he had seized, by his private authority, what the Senate, at Cicero's motion, confirmed to him, the most extraordinary command which had been granted to any man, he declared himself an enemy to all extraordinary commissions, in what hands so ever they were lodged.

This was prompted by the long letter of criticism which Brutus addressed to Cicero. This letter, which aroused Thomas Gordon's enthusiastic admiration, produced a very different effect on Middleton. He saw in it 'a churlish and morose arrogance, claiming infinite honours for himself, yet allowing none to anybody else, insolently chiding and dictating to one as much superior to him in wisdom as he was in years; the whole turning upon that romantic maxim of the Stoics enforced without any regard to times and circumstances: that a wise man has sufficiency of all things within himself.'[3] Middleton's *Cicero* was widely read and for those who read it the traditional view of Brutus as a model of Roman virtue would inevitably be weakened.

Among those who read it was the young Edward Gibbon,[4] who wrote in 1765–6 a 'Character of Brutus' (published posthumously in 1814) which shows that to him too Brutus was very far from being a hero or a model of virtue. After observing that 'the Memory of Caesar, celebrated as it is, has not been transmitted down to posterity with such uniform and encreasing applause as that of his PATRIOT ASSASSIN', he goes on to ask, 'in what consisted THE DIVINE VIRTUE of Brutus'. His answer amounts to a strong condemnation of the patriot assassin. 'The Design of the younger Brutus was vast and perhaps impracticable, the Execution feeble and unfortunate. Neither as a Statesman nor as a General did Brutus ever approve himself equal to the arduous task he had so rashly undertaken, of restoring the Commonwealth; instead of restoring it, the Death of a mild and generous Usurper produced only a series of Civil Wars, and the Reign of three Tyrants whose union and whose discord was alike fatal to the Roman People.' Turning to Brutus's personal character Gibbon finds his reputation for virtue belied by his dealings with the Salaminians, an example of 'unrelenting avarice' hardly to be paralleled among the misdeeds of Verres, and by his acceptance of office from and his oath of allegiance to the man whom he was soon to kill.[5]

The most influential nineteenth-century historians of Rome, Niebuhr and Mommsen, both stopped short of the death of Caesar. Niebuhr did not get beyond the first Punic War and was in any case primarily interested in origins and in institutions. Mommsen's work is more relevant to our theme, for though it ends at a point two years before the Ides of March, his treatment of Caesar and other leading figures of his age makes it clear that if he had carried his story further he would have shown little sympathy with Caesar's assassins. Mommsen's admiration for Caesar was, however, nothing new in Germany. A similar attitude is found in Wilhelm Drumann, professor of history at Königsberg, who published in 1834 to 1844 an elaborate history of the transition from Republic to Empire in the form of a series of biographies of the men of the period. Drumann combined a thorough and scholarly study of the sources with a very definite point of view. He ended his preface with the words: 'Without my intending it, though not contrary to my wishes, my book is a eulogy of monarchy, and I rejoice at the unintended result, which for me does not apply only to Roman history, for the Prussian subject of a Friedrich Wilhelm can have no other political faith than [and here he quotes the Greek of Herodotus] "monarchy is best".'[6]

This being his view, it is not surprising that he has little sympathy with the man who killed one whom he regarded as the greatest of the Romans. He represents Brutus as a dreamer out of touch with reality. 'The gap between reality and his ideals grew ever wider; misfortune changed his earnestness into melancholy; the solitude of night, in which, lacking a firm foundation of belief and understanding, he sought for a solution of the difficulties of the day, plunged him ever deeper into reverie. Overstrained and in a state of nervous excitement he saw visions. Finally, disillusioned about virtue he abandoned everything and died in a terrible state of mind.' With no judgment or knowledge of the world, he was constantly disappointed by events. For all his learning he was incapable of understanding the needs of contemporary society. He was an obstinate rather than a strong man, a man who could be influenced, as he was by Cassius, and one whose conviction of his own righteousness did not prevent him from sacrificing what was right to the illusory ideal of his country's freedom.[7]

Drumann's depreciation of Brutus was echoed in German historians of the later nineteenth century. Wilhelm Ihne (or rather A. W. Zumpt, who was largely responsible for the final volume of Ihne's *Römische Geschichte* published in 1890) described him as one of those men whose inner weakness belies the impressive appearance they present to the world, men who arouse the highest hopes but always disappoint them. Another scholar of the same period, Gardthausen, depicts a Brutus who was of all men the least suited for the deed he undertook, a man of a contemplative rather than an energetic nature. He imagines him brooding over the idea of assassination, which slowly took hold of him and became a kind of nightmare obsession from which only the deed of bloodshed could free him. His 'iron mask hid a weak face'. He had none of the self-confidence and practical outlook of Caesar; he was 'a small man who felt himself obliged to be a great man'.[8]

It was not only happy subjects of the Prussian monarchy like Drumann who admired Caesar and criticized his murderers. Even in England with its traditions of freedom it is hard to find a good word said for Brutus in the nineteenth-century historians of Rome. The first of any note among these was Thomas Arnold. His *History* reached no further than the end of the Punic wars, but his views on the later period can be found in some articles he contributed to an encyclopaedia in 1823 to 1827, which were republished as a book after his death. Arnold was a liberal, but he was above all a moralist, and he condemns both Caesar and his murderers. He admires Caesar's intellect but not his moral character. 'Never,' he writes, 'did any man occasion so large an amount of human misery, with so little provocation.' Yet in spite of all his crimes, the circumstances of his death make him almost an object of compassion. 'We naturally sympathize with the victim, when the murderers, by having abetted or countenanced his offences, had deprived themselves of all just title to punish them, and when his fall was only accomplished by the treachery of assassination.'[9]

The first English historian of the nineteenth century to deal with the later Republic in any detail was Charles Merivale, who published in 1850–62 his *History of the Romans under the Empire*, which began with the period of Sulla. For him the later Republic was the prelude to Empire, and it is perhaps not surprising that he emphasized its weaknesses. He had a strong admiration for Caesar and a correspondingly low opinion of the Roman aristocracy of his day. His judgment of Brutus is severe. He 'had been the last to join, the earliest to desert, the unfurled banner of the Republic. Nor did he blush to govern Cisalpine Gaul for Caesar while his uncle still held Utica against him. A feeble panegyric of the sturdy sage whom he had abandoned while he affected to adopt his principles and emulate his practice, seemed to Brutus a sufficient tribute to his virtues.' Porcia was 'a woman of more masculine spirit than his own', but he 'failed nevertheless to acquire the firmness which nature had denied him'.[10] Brutus fares no better in George Long's *Decline of the Roman Republic* (1864–1874). Long turns the tables on the Republicans by claiming that it was they who were exercising a tyranny. Brutus and Cassius, so far from delivering their country from a usurper, committed wicked murder. As for Brutus's pretensions to virtue, 'few persons will affirm that a merciless money lender and extortioner can be a good man or a philosopher'. Perhaps he was 'a philosophical fanatic, who could reconcile contradictories, like those men whose profession of piety does not secure them against excessive love of money and other vices'.[11]

From the last quarter of the century we have two English biographies of Caesar, both aiming at a popular readership, those of J. A. Froude (1879) and W. Warde Fowler (1892). Both take a highly favourable view of Caesar and a correspondingly adverse one of the conspirators. Froude depicts Brutus as a fanatic, a man of 'gloomy habits, given to dreams and omens', and easily influenced. For Warde Fowler he is a weak man, prone to attach himself to stronger characters, with a narrow and feeble mind likely to go wrong in situations demanding cool judgment and the power to see things as they are. His lukewarm feelings were fanned into hatred of monarchy, and once persuaded 'he went into the plot with all the enthusiasm of weakness'.[12] A different point of view is that of the Dublin scholar L. C. Purser, who collaborated with R. Y. Tyrrell in an edition of Cicero's correspondence. His position is a little like that of Middleton in the eighteenth century. He had no great admiration for Caesar, but his study of Brutus in his relations with Cicero left him with a strong dislike of him as a man. He was an 'incomparable prig', 'austere, cold hearted, persistent and obdurate', a 'stiff and ungracious student who was educated beyond his powers in all sorts of fantastic Greek notions about the virtue of tyrannicide'. He was without practical wisdom and an incompetent general; even his philosophy 'did not become part and parcel of his nature'. Plutarch's statement, which we have seen reason to doubt, that after Pharsalus he informed Caesar of Pompey's destination prompts the comment, 'Loyalty appears to have been a virtue unknown to Brutus. Dante was right to put him in the very jaws of Satan.'[13] The influence of Purser is evident in Heitland's treatment of Brutus in his *Roman Republic* (1909). Like Purser he seems to feel a positive dislike for the man, and with a partisanship rare in the modern academic writer he condemns him as a 'greedy capitalist' or dismisses him as poor spirited, helpless and hesitating, as a 'sham philosopher, self-conscious, shallow, solemn and vain' with his 'ill timed scruples and pompous rectitude'.[14]

According to Victor Duruy, historian of Rome and of France and Minister of Public Instruction in the French government from 1863 to 1869, the legend of Brutus, though much shaken in 'Caesarian Germany and free England', still persisted in France.[15] His history, first published in 1843–4 and later reissued in revised and enlarged form, must have done much to dispel the legend. He had a strong admiration for Caesar and a low opinion of the Roman Republic, which, he assured his readers, had nothing in common with Republicanism as understood in the nineteenth century, but was a system of anarchy and plunder under which freedom was restricted to a narrow oligarchy. As for Brutus, we have the familiar charges of weakness and fanaticism, and also one that was perhaps typical of the nineteenth century, that he tried to arrest an inevitable historical development. 'Brutus died despairing of liberty, philosophy and virtue, a just chastisement for the dreamer who had thwarted his age without perceiving it, for the man of meditation who, thinking to stop with a dagger thrust a revolution which had been gathering for more than a century, had only succeeded in letting loose fearful calamities upon his country.'[16]

Duruy assures his readers that his views had not changed since his first edition of the 1840s. The assurance was to the point, for after Louis Napoleon's coup d'état of 1851 and the revival of empire Caesarism became something like orthodoxy in France. Another Frenchman R. T. Troplong, who had passed as a liberal but became Louis Napoleon's admirer and apologist, published in 1865 an essay on the fall of the Roman Republic highly favourable to Caesar, which looked very much like a justification of the new French emperor.[17] Duruy himself assisted Napoleon III in the writing of his *History of Julius Caesar* (1855–6), a work designed to show that Caesar, like the first Napoleon (and by implication the third), was the providential saviour of society.

Brutus, however, still had his admirers among the French intelligentsia of the mid-nineteenth century. Among these was Taine, who wrote that if anyone doubted Brutus's nobleness of heart and the justice of his cause, 'I would beg him to reread the admirable letter in which he reproaches Cicero for having recommended him to the benevolence of Octavius. There is nothing in antiquity more proud, generous, worthy of a free man, nothing which shows more sincerity, lack of self-interest, patriotic devotion; there is nothing more simple, solid, well reasoned, the reverse of the style of a fanatic and an enthusiast. Cato and Brutus may have stood for the past; but at least they stood for virtue.'[18]

Another French writer paints a picture of Brutus which if not exactly admiring is at least sympathetic. In addition to his other historical works Michelet wrote a *History of the Roman Republic*, in which he approached Brutus rather in the spirit of the creative writer, the dramatist or novelist, who relies on imagination and sympathy to reconstruct the thoughts and feelings of men of the past. His Brutus is a pathetic, even tragic, figure, not particularly gifted intellectually, but 'an ardent soul, elevated by Stoicism', with 'a certain ruggedness, something strange and eccentric, a fierce yearning for effort, for painful sacrifices'. He is sensitive, scrupulous, hesitating, tormented by the conflict between his obligations to Caesar and his political ideals. In his final period the necessities of war bring further torment and strain. 'Troubled, and, as it were, terrified, he demanded repose and strength of mind from that philosophy which had already imposed on him so many cruel sacrifices.' In spite of himself he was driven to violent acts and it was 'not surprising that he wished at any price to terminate this unhappy struggle, which had cost him humanity, friendship, ease of conscience, and which was gradually depriving him of his virtue'.[19] Less imaginative and better founded on the evidence is the study of Brutus by Gaston Boissier in his *Cicéron et ses amis*, first published in 1865. This does justice to his idealism and the strength of his philosophic convictions as well as to his personal charm, and at the same time recognizes his limitations and, as we have seen in the passage quoted in an earlier chapter, stresses the obstinacy which went with his single-mindedness.

In the present century there has been something of a reaction against the depreciation of Brutus so common in the nineteenth century. In Germany Matthias Gelzer, in his authoritative article on Brutus in Pauly-Wissowa's *Real-Encyclopädie*, gives a favourable picture of him, representing him as an unusually gifted member of the Roman nobility, admittedly limited in his outlook, but standing out among his contemporaries by virtue of his sincerity and the strength of his convictions.[20] Turning to this country and to the views of its academic world as represented by the *Cambridge Ancient History*, we find a summing-up of Brutus's character by M. P. Charlesworth which, though decidedly cool, is not hostile; to Charlesworth he was 'no unfair specimen of the late Republican senator', admired for his firmness of character and loyalty to an ideal, but with an intellectual equipment in no way superior to that of his fellow nobles. What of the action which won him his fame? For the Ides of March we turn to another volume of the *History* and a different author, F. E. Adcock. To him tyrannicide is merely a 'dull simplification'. So much for the deed which has made Brutus a hero to some and an object of execration to others.[21]

In the late 1930s there appeared two full-length books on Brutus, one by a Frenchman, Gérard Walter, the other by an American, Max Radin.[22] Walter did no more than tell the story without passing judgment on men and events. In his preface he described Brutus as the most modern of the ancients and as a kind of combination of Hamlet and Robespierre, but there is nothing in his text to explain and justify these paradoxes. Radin's aim was 'to present a living person and not a symbol' and he assumed that Brutus was 'not essentially different from living persons whom we know'. He considered that the old attitude which made a hero of him had more in its favour than the more recent one of disparagement. He saw him as a man of ability with a capacity for leadership, humane by the standards of his day, ready to undertake new tasks and to adapt himself to new situations. But though he showed a marked capacity for political activity his heart was not in it; he was by nature a student. It was unfortunate for him that he felt irresistibly drawn to Cato, with the result that the Ides of March and Philippi were 'the realization of a purpose that was not his own'. He was 'an incurably cleft soul'.[23]

In the same year as Radin's book there appeared a much more substantial and influential work of scholarship, Ronald Syme's *Roman Revolution*. This is mainly concerned with the rise to power of Augustus and the establishment of his principate, and it treats him with marked severity. Caesar is more favourably treated, but Brutus also gets some quite warm commendation. For Syme he and Caesar each had right on his side. Brutus was a man of 'firm character and Roman patriotism' and a 'sincere and consistent champion of legality'; he and the others who fought at Philippi fought for 'a principle, a tradition and a class – narrow, imperfect and outworn, but for all that the soul and spirit of Rome'. To condemn them because they failed is simply to judge by results. And yet for Syme himself 'in the end the principate has to be accepted'. It is difficult to get away from 'the verdict of history'.[24]

Syme's outlook was clearly coloured by the contemporary European situation, by the rise of tyrannies more baleful than that of Caesar, the threat of armed force, the loss of freedom in some countries and the fear of its loss in others. Walter deliberately refrained from anything that would suggest contemporary events; Radin, writing in the United States, showed no signs of being influenced by the politics of Europe. 'We do not now justify assassination,' he writes, 'even of indubitable tyrants.'[25] If he had written a few years later he might have thought differently. If the plot to assassinate Hitler had succeeded, even a strict political moralist might have been willing to approve. Assassination may still be justifiable as a last resort. And yet having said that one remembers how often it has been misused against those who can by no stretch of the imagination be called tyrants. One remembers too that those involved in the plot against Hitler, like Brutus honourable men, like him, though in a different way, failed to achieve their object. There cannot have been many cases of assassination that have been both morally justifiable and beneficial in their results. That of Caesar cannot be included among them, if only because it fails on the second count, while its moral justification, in spite of the approval of 'Rome's least mortal mind', Cicero, remains doubtful.

The Justice of the memorable Ides of March [wrote Gibbon] has been a subject of Controversy above eighteen hundred Years, and will so remain, as long as the interests of the Community shall be considered by different Tempers in different Lights. Men of high and active Spirits, who deem the Loss of Liberty, or sometimes in other words the Loss of Power, the worst of misfortunes, will approve the use of every Stratagem and every Weapon in the Chace of the common Foe of Society . . . On the other hand the Lovers of Order and Moderation, who are swayed by the Calm of Reason, rather than by the impetuosity of Passion, will never consent to establish every private Citizen the Judge and Avenger of the public Injury.[26]

Lovers of order and moderation might perhaps feel better disposed to Brutus than Gibbon suggests, for it was he who stood for the old constitution and Caesar who treated it without respect. The sympathies of the liberal and the democrat will naturally be with those who stood for free and open government as opposed to an autocracy based on armed force. On the other hand, admirers of strong men and authoritarian government are naturally drawn to Caesar, while a radical or socialist, remembering that Caesar was a reformer and one of the *populares*, the party of the people, might be disposed to side with him and to depreciate his assassins as a group of reactionary noblemen concerned only to maintain their own privileges.[27] *Utcumque ferent ea facta minores.* The doubts which Virgil voiced about Lucius Brutus apply no less to Marcus.

CHAPTER THREE

BRUTUS IN LITERATURE

I SHAKESPEARE AND HIS PREDECESSORS

How many ages hence
Shall this our lofty scene be acted over
In states unborn and accents yet unknown.

So Cassius in Shakespeare's *Julius Caesar*. The Ides of March was
indeed a fit subject for drama. It was an exciting story, with plenty
of incident. It involved great personages and high moral and
political issues. Human relationships were involved as well as
political ideals. There were the different personalities and different
motives of the two chief conspirators, Brutus and Cassius; there
was the relationship of Caesar to Brutus, one of friendship, with the
possibility of an even closer tie, that of paternity. Though there
was no love interest in the usual sense, there were female characters,
Caesar's wife Calpurnia and Brutus's wife Porcia, to add variety
and sentiment. Latin literature provided models for tragedy in the
plays of Seneca, and there was precedent in antiquity for drama
based on incidents from Roman history. It is therefore not surprising that with the growth of a knowledge of and admiration for
ancient Rome attempts were made to dramatize Caesar's death.

The earliest of these was that of M. A. Muret (Muretus), written
in Latin in 1544 when he was only eighteen. It was acted, along
with the Latin plays of George Buchanan on biblical themes, at the
Collège de Guyenne at Bordeaux, and Montaigne, who was a
pupil there, took a leading part. As one would expect of a scholar
writing at that date and in those circumstances, the play follows the
precepts of Horace and the practice of Seneca. It consists of five
short acts separated by choral odes. Caesar's death takes place

off stage, and we pass from the scene where Decimus Brutus persuades him to come to the Senate in spite of Calpurnia's forebodings to one in which Brutus and Cassius inform the people that Caesar is dead and Rome is free. Finally the dead Caesar appears, to announce his ascent to the stars and the future punishment of the murderers. The chorus, not without ancient precedent, veers from one side to the other. When Brutus and Cassius have decided to kill the tyrant they express approval and claim that Jupiter also approves, but after the assassination they are equally ready to condemn the sacrilegious act, and they greet the appearance of the deified Caesar with the assurance that a reward in heaven awaits the virtuous.

The first play in the vernacular on the Ides of March was the *César*, sometimes referred to as *La Mort de César*, of Jacques Grévin, written in 1558, when he was twenty years old.[1] Grévin had been a pupil of Muret at the Collège de Boncourt in Paris, and his play is based on Muret's, but it is much longer and has a number of original features. For Muret's impersonal chorus Grévin substituted one consisting of Caesar's soldiers speaking individually, and as one would expect, they do not, as Muret's chorus had done, express approval of the conspirators' intentions. The play ends not with the appearance of the deified Caesar followed by approving comments from the chorus, but more realistically with Antony addressing the soldiers and stirring them up to vengeance. The political message of the play, if there is one, is far from clear. Its last words, put in the mouth of one of the soldiers, are 'Ceste mort est fatale/Aux nouveaux inventeurs de puissance Royale', but otherwise there is no sign of bias in favour of Republicanism.

In Italy a play in the vernacular on the death of Caesar was published in 1594, Orlando Pescetti's *Il Cesare*. Pescetti gives more space than Muret and Grévin to the deliberations of Brutus and Cassius, but there is not much attempt at characterization. Brutus takes the lead throughout. He has already decided on tyrannicide when the play opens, and though Pescetti includes Cassius's attempt to make him kill Antony, there is little differentiation between the two conspirators, and both give utterance to the same sort of commonplaces about the blessings of liberty and the evils of tyranny. The play ends with one chorus, consisting of citizens, praising Brutus and liberty and another, of soldiers, lamenting the death of Caesar and threatening war; a messenger paints a gloomy picture of the fate of Rome, and the chorus utters some final reflections on the changes and chances of life. Though the play itself does not show any bias in favour of one or the other party, the dedication, which compares its recipient the Duke of Ferrara to Caesar, shows that Pescetti was no propagandist for republican liberty, as does the prologue, in which Venus reveals to Mars that Caesar is to be killed by sacrilegious hands and Jupiter promises a place in heaven for him and punishment for his murderers.

Pescetti's play, like those of Muret and Grévin, was about the death of Caesar, and though Brutus inevitably played an important part, he was not the chief character. Moreover, so long as the classical unities were observed the story could not be carried on to Philippi and Brutus's death. The Florentine Giannotti, however, whom we have already met as a supporter of republicanism, had the idea of writing a tragedy of Brutus with the scene laid at Philippi. In 1533 he sent an outline of the plot to Lorenzo Strozzi, inviting his cooperation. He explained that he had departed from the historical facts in several respects. He had brought Porcia and Cassius's wife Junia to Philippi, and had made Junia commit suicide as well as Porcia, while Brutus was made to kill himself on the battlefield. The tragedy, if it was ever completed, has not survived.[2] Another sixteenth-century play which deals with events after Caesar's death is Robert Garnier's *Porcie* of 1592, in which, as the title shows, the chief character is Brutus's wife and the climax is her suicide after hearing the news of his death. But as Brutus himself does not appear at all in it the play hardly concerns us. By contrast with it the Latin tragedy on the death of Brutus by a young German scholar Michael Virdung, published in 1596, left Porcia out completely.[3] This is a short and simple work, with only two important characters, Brutus and Antony, and very little incident. Cassius is already dead when the play opens with the appearance of the ghost of Caesar. Brutus's decision to attack is announced to Antony in the third act, and in the fourth he puts an end to his life. The final act breaks off in the middle of a line and appears to be unfinished. Undramatic, academic, and inexpert as it is, the play has a certain interest on account of its apparently wholehearted approval of Brutus and his ideals; the chorus has nothing but admiration for the patriot champion of liberty and abhorrence for the would-be enslavers of their country, Antony and Octavian.

In England the unities were little regarded and the anonymous *Tragedie of Caesar and Pompey*, or *Caesar's Revenge*,[4] believed to date from the last decade of the sixteenth century, begins at Pharsalia, includes the murder of Pompey in Egypt, Caesar's encounter with Cleopatra, and Cato's suicide at Utica, as well as the death of Caesar, and ends with the battle of Philippi. According to the title page of the 1607 edition, the play was acted privately by the students of Trinity College, Oxford, and its many learned references suggest an academic origin. Brutus might be called the dramatic hero since he appears with Pompey in the first scene and the play ends with his death; but the crowded scenes leave no room for the development of character. In the opening scene Brutus is hailed by Pompey as

> second hope of sad oppressed Rome,
> In whome the ancient *Brutus* vertue shines,
> That purchast first the *Romaine* liberty,

but in the last act he repents of his ingratitude to Caesar. So far as it is not a digest of Roman history, the theme of the play is revenge. At Philippi Brutus is haunted by the ghost of Caesar, which denounces him as traitor and homicide and threatens vengeance, and when he kills himself the ghost's comment is, 'Murther by her owne guilty hand doth bleed.'

More in accordance with classical models was *The Tragedy of Julius Caesar* by the Scotsman Sir William Alexander, published in 1609. This is very much a production of the study rather than the theatre. Alexander was a learned man, well versed in classical literature, and his characters are all too much given to displaying his learning. The goddess Juno makes a lengthy speech by way of prologue: the chorus utters sententious platitudes; the murder of Caesar takes place off stage and is announced to Calpurnia by a messenger. The play is entirely without life. Brutus does not play a particularly important part and his character is not clearly delineated. Nor does any political message emerge. The chorus utters some praises of liberty, but Alexander, who followed James VI to

England, tutored his sons and was given an earldom, can have had no intention of glorifying tyrannicide.

His play dates from a few years after the first performance of Shakespeare's *Julius Caesar*, but he is unlikely to have known it, as it was not printed until the First Folio of 1623. If he had, he would probably have thought it sadly lacking in learning, and would have condemned its failure to observe the canons of classical drama. To the modern reader a comparison of his play with Shakespeare's is more likely to suggest that it is an advantage to a dramatist to have small Latin and less Greek. Alexander's work and that of the earlier playwrights who handled similar themes show by contrast Shakespeare's originality and dramatic power. None of them can have had a wide appeal, whereas Shakespeare's play was and remained popular. Previous playwrights, apart from the author of the *Tragedie of Caesar and Pompey*, had been bound by classical precedent; Shakespeare ignored it. They were learned men; he had little classical erudition, but made up for his lack of it by his understanding of human character. He treated the actors in the drama as men and women like ourselves, with the result that we feel ourselves to be in ancient Rome in a way that we do not with the works of more learned writers. It matters not in the least that there is no ancient authority for the sweaty nightcaps of the Roman populace, much less for Brutus's striking clock.

Shakespeare's only, or only important, source was Plutarch, whom he knew from North's version of Amyot's French translation. He used the lives of Caesar, Brutus and Antony; and unhampered by respect for the unities he carried on the story from the Ides of March to Philippi, selecting significant incidents and avoiding the mistake of trying to get in too much. His characterization owes something to Plutarch, with his liking for personal details and his sympathetic interest in all his subjects, but he develops in his own way the material provided by his source, and where, as in the case of Casca, Plutarch gave him little more than a name, draws on his own invention to create a new character. Among the actors in the drama Brutus stands out. Julius Caesar gives his name to the play, but he is killed half way through, and during the first half he is off the stage for more than three-quarters of the time. Brutus is the hero of the play.

At his first appearance we find him worried and withdrawn. Cassius reproaches him for his coolness towards him, and here Shakespeare makes a slight but significant departure from his source. According to Plutarch the two men were temporarily alienated because of their rival claims to the city praetorship and Cassius resented Caesar's preference of Brutus to himself. Shakespeare makes no mention of the praetorship or of Cassius's resentment. It is Brutus who shows a lack of friendliness, and the cause of this is nothing external and specific, but rather Brutus's preoccupations; he neglects his friend because he is 'with himself at war'. What is on his mind he does not reveal, but we can easily guess that he is concerned about the state of Rome under Caesar. He is ready to respond to Cassius's promptings, and at the end of the first act, as Cassius says, 'three parts of him is ours'.

When in the second act he is found in his orchard soliloquizing he has decided on action, but the decision has brought him no relief.

> Between the acting of a dreadful thing
> And the first motion, all the interim is
> Like a phantasma or a hideous dream.

When the conspirators come in to meet him he shows another side to his character, his high-minded idealism. He rejects Cassius's suggestion that they should bind themselves with an oath (Plutarch had recorded that there was no oath, but did not attribute this to Brutus), and, more important for the future, he refuses to allow the slaughter of Antony along with Caesar. After the conspirators depart he calls to his slave boy Lucius, but finding him fast asleep forbears to waken him. It is a small incident but significant; Shakespeare, on his own account and without Plutarch's authority, makes Brutus kind and considerate to his slave.[5] In the next scene too we see the human side of his character. He is an affectionate husband as well as a kindly slave master; the part which Porcia, or Portia as she appears in Shakespeare, plays was given by Plutarch, but the loving words which Brutus addresses to her are Shakespeare's own addition.

For the assassination of Caesar Shakespeare follows the story as told by Plutarch (though 'et tu Brute' must come indirectly from

Suetonius), but after Caesar is killed he departs rather far from his source. On Brutus's proposal the conspirators bathe their hands in Caesar's blood, a melodramatic act with no authority in Plutarch, which seems out of keeping with Brutus as he is portrayed elsewhere in the play. Then, when one would expect him to proceed to the forum and proclaim the restoration of freedom the action is held up by the arrival first of Antony's servant, then of Antony himself. Antony now comes to the fore, 'a shrewd contriver', to quote Cassius's words, in his flattery of Brutus, but also warmhearted and genuinely grieved at Caesar's death. Brutus now shows the trustful, indeed naive, side of his character. He welcomes Antony and at once accedes to his request to be allowed to make a funeral speech for Caesar. When Cassius demurs he reassures him by saying that he himself will address the people first and will inform them that Antony speaks with his permission. This he believes will be to his advantage rather than the reverse, and he is quite happy with Antony's promise not to blame the conspirators but only to speak well of Caesar.

The scene in the forum where Brutus and Antony in turn address the people is one of Shakespeare's most brilliant. He knew from Plutarch that Antony had delivered a funeral speech, had informed the people of the contents of Caesar's will, and had displayed his body to them. He knew too that Brutus had previously addressed the people on different occasions with varying success. For his own dramatic purposes he made a speech by Brutus immediately precede that of Antony, and the contrasting oratory of the two men is his own creation. The short sentences which he puts into the mouth of Brutus were presumably suggested by what Plutarch says about the laconic brevity of his Greek letters, but the speech is by no means a blunt, straightforward utterance. It is carefully composed, and could well be described in the words Cicero used of his speech on the Capitol – 'a most elegant composition, which could not be bettered as regards sentiments and words' but lacked the fire he himself would have put into it.[6] Shakespeare probably did not know of these comments or of the other evidence for Brutus's oratory; instinct has guided him as surely as scholarship could have done.

After the speeches in the forum and the murder of Cinna the poet there is another scene in Rome which serves to introduce Octavius, and we then move to Brutus's camp at Sardis. This was the scene of his quarrel with Cassius, and it is in keeping with Shakespeare's strong interest in character that he chose this incident for extended treatment. He wisely made the condemnation of Lucius Pella precede and not, as it does in Plutarch, follow the quarrel, and so provided a specific ground for the alienation of the two men. But what is remarkable is that he seems to do his best to enlist his audience's sympathies in favour of Cassius. Brutus was in the right from the point of view of strict morality; Cassius had the reputation of being hot-tempered, and Plutarch was inclined to be biased against him. Yet in Shakespeare it is Brutus who loses his temper and Cassius who suffers under his reproaches. After they have made it up, however, we learn the reason for Brutus's behaviour; he has heard of the death of Portia. Shakespeare has linked the news of her suicide, which Plutarch recorded at the very end of his story, with the quarrel. Brutus, though trying to take the news stoically, is really 'sick of many griefs', and his unreasonable behaviour to Cassius is easily understood and forgiven when we learn of the sorrow which afflicts him and which he is trying to suppress.

Beautifully managed though the scene is, one cannot but regret that Shakespeare chose to include the intervention of the unnamed poet. In Plutarch it is Favonius who breaks in. He quotes a line of Homer which North turned into a doggerel couplet, and hence he was transformed by Shakespeare into a poet. And whereas in Plutarch his intervention puts an end to the quarrel, in Shakespeare the two leaders are already reconciled when he comes in, and his appearance has little point. We may also have some doubts, as most commentators have had, about the second announcement of Portia's death, made by Messala immediately after the quarrel scene. Is this a case of a doublet, of two alternative versions which have somehow survived in the text? Certainly it seems inconsistent with dramatic economy that the news should be announced when Brutus knows it already. If, however, the text as we have it does represent Shakespeare's final and considered version, the intention must be to emphasize the outward mask of philosophic indifference under which Brutus hides his distress. He is now the public man, the leader, who must, as Cicero had said in his letter of condolence, set an example in not giving way to his emotions.

The scene in which the apparition appears to Brutus nicely balances that in his orchard at the beginning of the second Act. Once more it is night; once more Brutus is alone with his drowsy slave Lucius and as before he shows an affectionate consideration for the boy. The apparition is described as Caesar's ghost in the stage directions, and towards the end of the play Brutus reveals that Caesar has appeared to him a second time at Philippi. This perhaps helps to give unity to the play by stressing the continued influence of Caesar after his death; but when the apparition appears it announces itself as Brutus's 'evil spirit', and there is nothing in the text to identify it with Caesar. In Brutus's encounter with his evil spirit Shakespeare makes a slight but significant expansion of Plutarch. In reply to a question the apparition says that Brutus will see him at Philippi. 'Well,' says Brutus, 'then I shall see thee again?' 'Ay, at Philippi,' is the answer, to which Brutus rejoins with 'Why, I will see thee at Philippi then. Now I have taken heart thou vanishest.' The brief hesitation, and the question before Brutus accepts the challenge show him a little less self-confident than he appears in Plutarch.

The interview between Brutus and Cassius before the battle of Philippi in which they decide to end their lives in the case of defeat is sadly mismanaged by Shakespeare, thanks to a mistranslation by North which gave the impression that Brutus still disapproved of suicide and had not changed his mind since he criticized Cato, which is the reverse of what Plutarch says. Shakespeare was content to versify the unintelligible remarks which North attributed to Brutus, and the interview ends with him saying farewell and adding the lame and uncharacteristic lines: 'If we do meet again, why, we shall smile. If not, why then this parting was well made.' Nor does Shakespeare quite rise to the occasion when he comes to Brutus's suicide. In the crowded last act he is left with little room for extended treatment, and the final speech which he puts into Brutus's mouth seems a little perfunctory. Moreover, he makes Brutus, what he is not in Plutarch's story, meditative, tearful, weary of life. Shakespeare's Brutus, one might say, is more a Dane than an antique Roman.

When Shakespeare made Antony describe Brutus as the noblest Roman of them all, the only disinterested one among the conspirators, he was basing himself on Plutarch. The lines that follow are his own:

> His life was gentle; and the elements
> So mixed in him, that Nature might stand up,
> And say to all the world 'This was a man.'

We must suppose that Shakespeare had attempted to draw a character of whom this could justly be said. And yet some have found his Brutus a disagreeable person, 'pompous, opinionated and self-righteous', to quote one commentator.[7] These are certainly qualities for which there is some evidence in the ancient sources; but anyone coming to Shakespeare from those sources is likely to find his Brutus more human, more sensitive, less sure of himself, and to that extent more attractive, than the historical Brutus. Another criticism that has been made of Shakespeare's character is that his decision to kill Caesar is inadequately motivated, and certainly his rather tortuous soliloquy 'It must be by his death . . .' gives no clear idea of what he hoped to gain by assassination. Shakespeare's interest was not in the political issues. He is unlikely to have had much understanding of or sympathy with the ideals of Roman republicanism, and he had no desire to give a warning to tyrants and to encourage assassination. At the same time he does not condemn the murder of Caesar; we hear nothing of the wrath of heaven against the sacrilegious parricide. Brutus fails in the end, but he does so not because he has committed a wicked act, but because of his own weaknesses, or perhaps we should rather say because of his very virtues. Shakespeare's primary interest is in the characters rather than in their political aims, and it is Brutus's character that determines the outcome. Sensitive, scrupulous and high-minded, he is no match for his enemies; his generosity and trustfulness, his confidence in the rightness of his cause, lead to his failure. If there is a political lesson to be drawn from the play it is that idealism is not enough. As Hazlitt put it, 'Those who mean well themselves think well of others, and fall a prey to their security. That humanity and honesty which dispose men to resist injustice and tyranny render them unfit to cope with the cunning and power of those who are opposed to them.'[8]

2 FROM SHAKESPEARE TO THE PRESENT DAY

Shakespeare's *Julius Caesar* continued to hold the stage after his death and later English dramatists who took their material from ancient Rome did not attempt to rival him by new plays on Caesar and Brutus, but chose other themes. There is however one exception to this. In 1722 a curious attempt was made to improve on Shakespeare when John Sheffield, Duke of Buckingham, rewrote *Julius Caesar* as two plays, *The Tragedy of Julius Caesar* and *The Tragedy of Marcus Brutus*. The first of these is fairly close to Shakespeare, though with additions and verbal alterations, always for the worse. The second is more independent. The scene is laid first at Athens, then at Philippi, and there is some love interest. Cassius's wife Junia is with him at Athens (on the day before the battle of Philippi); a young Roman, Varius, harbours a hopeless passion for her, and a chorus of youths and virgins utters an ode, contributed by Pope, on the blessings of married love. Even if Buckingham's implied criticism of Shakespeare, that he made one play out of what should have been two, is legitimate, his own work is so inept that it is impossible to take him seriously. Its quality can be illustrated by some lines from the beginning and from the end of the *Tragedy of Marcus Brutus*. After announcing that the scene is Athens the prologue goes on:

> Amidst all these ye shall behold a man
> The most applauded since mankind began;
> Out-shining ev'n those Greeks who most excel:
> Whose life was one fix'd course of doing well.

And at the end of the play one of Brutus's friends praises him in the words:

> If public virtue well be understood
> Here was the greatest man that e'er was good.

To which the other side rejoins with a slightly better couplet:

> Yet the great Gods a righteous judgment send;
> He lov'd his country, but he kill'd his friend.

Of dramatic writers after Shakespeare the only one to my knowledge who followed him in including both the murder of Caesar and the death of Brutus was Herder. In 1774 he wrote a cantata, or lyric drama for music, with the title *Brutus*; after he had applied in vain to Gluck it was set to music by J. C. F. Bach, one of the sons of Johann Sebastian, who was Konzertmeister at Bückeburg where Herder was living. Herder made no great claims for the work; without the music, he said, it was a mere framework, and the best features in it were not his own but came from either Shakespeare or history.[1] Shakespeare perhaps more than history, and Shakespeare romanticized. Herder's *Brutus* is certainly not classical in spirit.

His lyrical outpourings contrast with the lifeless prose of the contemporary German Swiss writer J. J. Bodmer, author of no fewer than three plays concerning Brutus, *Marcus Brutus, Julius Caesar* and *Brutus und Kassius Tod*.[2] These plays were not intended for the stage and are devoid of dramatic merit. They were intended primarily to inculcate political ideals, to inspire patriotism and hatred of tyranny. In *Julius Caesar* (1763) Caesar is depicted as a despot above the laws, happy to be addressed as sultan by Antony; he despises the people, his clemency is a pretence, and he is unhappy so long as anyone lives who wants a republic. In the play on the death of Brutus and Cassius (1782) Bodmer conscientiously follows Plutarch and for good measure introduces Horace and the younger Cicero. Brutus is depicted as a man of fine character. At the beginning of the play Cicero's son describes him as one whose inflexible uprightness is founded on principle, and confesses that he would be tempted to think ill of Jupiter if he allowed this 'godlike man' to be defeated. After Brutus's suicide Octavius pays a tribute to him in a prosaic paraphrase of the last speech of Antony in Shakespeare's play, but with the unShakespearian addition that it was 'Katonische Fanatisme' which had made him kill his benefactor. Bodmer had some reservations about Brutus; the play ends with Messala joining Octavius convinced that the only way to end bloodshed is for Rome to be under one master.

France, however, rather than Germany or Switzerland was the home of classical drama, and in France of the seventeenth and eighteenth centuries at least five plays were produced which had as their subject either the death of Caesar or that of Brutus. They all observe the unities, and until the last and best of them, Voltaire's *La Mort de César*, none shows any sign of Shakespearian influence.

La Mort de César by Georges de Scudéry, first performed in 1635,[3] is notable for its bias in favour of Caesar and against his assassins. It is dedicated to Cardinal Richelieu, who is exhorted to imitate Caesar, and in a prefatory address to the reader Scudéry anticipates criticism of his work by admirers of Brutus. He observes that even apart from the fact that he himself lives under a monarchy and not a republic he does not share their high opinion of Brutus; if he was so devoted to the liberty of his country he should have died after Pharsalia, and should certainly not have flattered Caesar and then become his assassin, 'or rather parricide'. Scudéry's Brutus is not an attractive character. He is insincere in his dealings with Caesar and indulges in abject flattery of him. In defiance of history he, rather than Decimus Brutus, is given the task of persuading Caesar to come to the Senate in spite of Calpurnia's forebodings, and he does so by hypocritical promises that he is to be made king. Caesar on the other hand is displayed as trusting and magnanimous, believing in Brutus's virtues and adhering to his policy of clemency in spite of pressure from Antony and Lepidus. In the last act Brutus and Cassius in defeatist mood decide to leave Rome and Antony stirs up the people in his funeral oration. Finally it is reported that Caesar has ascended into heaven and appeared there as a new star; a temple is to be erected to him so that everyone will know that he is numbered among the gods.

Scudéry's play was immediately followed by *La Mort de Brute et de Porcie* by Guion Guérin de Bouscal.[4] In this play the scene is laid at Philippi, and Porcia, with the inevitable confidante, is there as well as her husband. Apart from this the play follows Plutarch fairly closely. It ends with the death of Brutus, followed by that of Porcia, determined not to survive him. The scene alternates between Brutus's camp and that of Antony, and each leader dilates on the justice of his cause in long declamatory speeches, but the subtitle of the play, *La Vengeance de la Mort de César*, and the final words, in which Octavius claims that peace has been restored and vice put to flight, show where the author's sympathies lie. A rather better play on the same lines is *La Porcie Romaine* by Claude Boyer, produced in 1645.[5] Here too Porcia is with Brutus at Philippi (or rather Pharsalia, for Boyer, following some ancient writers, makes the two battles take place on the same site) and the play ends with the suicide of both. Boyer adds to the suspense by making Porcia first hear from Cassius the false news of Brutus's death, then learn that he is alive and victorious, after which he himself appears, defeated and determined on death. Brutus escapes captivity; Porcia faced by Octavius boldly defies him; finally we learn that both have put an end to their lives. Political issues are not to the fore; the emphasis is on human feelings. Brutus is depicted as a loving husband anxious for his wife but at the same time supported and encouraged by her. But as the title of the play shows it is Porcia rather than Brutus who is the centre of interest, and a Porcia who is a model of Roman virtue.

The next French dramatist to handle Brutus was a woman, Mlle Barbier, who returned to the theme of the Ides of March in *La Mort de César*, published in 1710. Not content with the conjugal affection of Brutus and Porcia she introduced a further love interest, boldly inventing where history failed her. She brought into the story a new female character (with confidante), Caesar's great niece Octavia, sister of the future Augustus. Antony (who did in fact marry her some years later) is in love with her, but Caesar, afraid of Brutus and anxious to win him over, plans to give her to him as wife and to transfer Porcia to Antony. This has the reverse effect, relieving Brutus of his loyalty to Caesar. He pretends however to agree; Porcia believes that he is going to leave her, but refuses to marry Antony. Octavia is willing to marry Brutus, but Antony is unwilling to give her up. Caesar remains obdurate for a time, but eventually relents and allows Antony to have Octavia and Brutus to keep Porcia. There are other complications. Caesar makes an enemy of Antony as well as of Brutus by his matrimonial plans. After these are given up Brutus informs him of the conspiracy against him and does his best to dissuade him from going to the Senate; it is only when Caesar accepts the diadem, the symbol of royalty, that he finally decides to join with the other conspirators. Mlle Barbier was criticized for representing Caesar as weak and timid and making Brutus greater than him.[6] Her Caesar certainly is weak, though there is nothing particularly admirable about her Brutus. But a play which departs so far from history and does so in such a silly fashion cannot be taken seriously as an interpretation of the characters involved and their actions.

Voltaire's play *La Mort de César* was completed in 1731 and performed privately in 1733 and again in 1735; the next year saw its first authorized publication, but it was not produced publicly on the stage until 1743. It originated in Voltaire's visit to England. While there he saw a performance of Shakespeare's *Julius Caesar*; he made a translation of Antony's funeral speech, and was urged to translate the whole play but declined. He regarded Shakespeare as a genius who lived in a barbarous age and whose plays were marred by the crudities of his times. Instead therefore of translating the 'monstrous work' (*l'ouvrage monstrueux*) of Shakespeare he wrote his own play, which he claimed was in the English manner. He incorporated Shakespeare's version of Antony's speech, but apart from this there is little Shakespearian about the play, and it is not easy to see in it the peculiarly English qualities which he ascribed to it, 'that strong love of liberty and those bold features which are rarely found in French writers.'[7]

So far from including some love interest as Mlle Barbier had done Voltaire dispenses entirely with female characters. Even Porcia is absent. This does not, however, mean that there is no sentiment. Voltaire accepts the story that Brutus was the son of Caesar, and bases his play on the relationship between the two and the conflict between the tie of blood and what Brutus regards as his patriotic duty. He had already written a play *Brutus* on the founder of the Roman Republic, who put his sons to death in the interests of state. He followed it by one on his supposed descendant who in Voltaire's version sacrifices his father to his political principles, and in support of his version he could point to the claim made by Brutus, writing to Cicero, that he would not allow even his father, should he return to life, to have more power than the laws and the senate.[8]

At the beginning of the play Caesar informs Antony that Brutus is his son by Servilia, who was secretly married to him and had signed a document in proof of his paternity. But Brutus,

> De nos antiques loix ce défenseur austère
> Ce rigide ennemi du pouvoir arbitraire,

is invincibly opposed to him. Caesar's feelings about him are mixed.

> *Il m'irrite, il me plaît. Son coeur indépendant*
> *Sur mes sens étonnés prend un fier ascendant.*
> *Sa fermeté m'impose, et je l'excuse même*
> *De condamner en moi l'autorité suprême.*

He hopes that Brutus will change his views when he learns of his relationship to Caesar. Meanwhile, however, Brutus's views harden in the other direction, and before he meets Caesar he has determined on killing him and has bound himself by an oath along with the other conspirators.

Caesar now reveals to Brutus that he is his son. The interview ends in deadlock. Brutus is at first overwhelmed by the news, but eventually bids Caesar, if he is indeed his father, to kill him on the spot or cease to reign. Caesar replies by disowning him.

> *J'apprendrai de Brutus à cesser d'être humain.*
> *Je ne le connais plus.*

Brutus informs the other conspirators that he is Caesar's son and shares his dilemma with them.

> *Pleurant d'être son fils, honteux de ses bienfaits;*
> *Admirant ses vertus, condamnant ses forfaits;*
> *Voyant en lui mon père, un coupable, un grand homme,*
> *Entrainé par César et retenu par Rome.*

But he reassures them that his resolve is unaltered.

> *J'embrasse avec horreur une vertu cruelle.*

There is a further scene, and a more emotional one, between Brutus and Caesar in which Caesar implores Brutus to be his son in reality and Brutus begs Caesar to renounce the royal diadem and to be not a king but a citizen. Each remains unmoved by the other and Brutus leaves in tears, weeping, as he says, for Caesar. He does not appear again. After the murder, which takes place off stage, it is Cassius who comes out and addresses the people. Voltaire seems to have lost interest in Brutus.

A little earlier than Voltaire's *Mort de César* an Italian man of letters, Antonio Conti, had written a play on the same well-worn theme, *Giulio Cesare*, completed in 1718 and published in 1726.

Not content with one play on the Ides of March, he followed it in 1744 with another, *Marco Bruto*, a second version written from the point of view not of Caesar but of Brutus. In the first play he emphasized Caesar's virtues rather than his vices, showing him, as he says in his preface, grand in his ideas, magnificent in his actions, liberal, alert, fertile in good plans, and prompt in executing them. Brutus puzzled him, with all his apparent contradictions and inconsistencies, but after some years he saw that it was possible to represent the same events in a different light, so as to win sympathy for Brutus; he now depicted him as actuated solely by love of his country, as a man whose singlemindedness contrasted with and corrected the less pure characters of the others involved, including Porcia, who has an important role in both plays and is represented as passionate and revengeful.[9]

More interesting than these worthy and conscientious but academic and rather lifeless productions is Alfieri's *Bruto Secondo*. In his memoirs Alfieri tells how he had seen Voltaire's *Brutus* some years before and remembered little of it, but hearing from his mistress the Countess of Albany about a performance of it which she had witnessed he decided to see what he could do on the same theme. He first wrote *Bruto Primo*, on the founder of the Roman Republic, then followed it with *Bruto Secondo*, on Marcus Brutus and the murder of Caesar. Though he does not say so in his memoirs, he must have known *La Mort de César* as well as *Brutus*, for his play is on the same lines as Voltaire's. In both Brutus is revealed to be Caesar's son and in both the main interest of the drama lies in their relationship and the attempts of each to win the other over. Alfieri undoubtedly improves on Voltaire. His play is better thought out, and his hatred of tyranny and devotion to the ideal of freedom give it a strong and consistent theme.

It begins with a meeting of the Senate at which Brutus boldly addresses Caesar and urges him to give up the idea of being king and assume the more glorious role of a citizen; as for himself, he does not love Caesar, because Caesar does not love Rome, nor does he hate him, because he does not fear him, and he does not fear him because he is always ready to die rather than to be a slave. Later in the play the two men have a private interview. Brutus believes that Caesar is not a tyrant at heart, and that he can still be reformed and as a private citizen can make Rome free, strong and vigorous. He takes the initiative at the interview, and his appeals to Caesar's better nature make some impression. Caesar acknowledges his admiration for Brutus, and indeed recognizes that there is some truth in what he says. If he were not Caesar he would wish to be Brutus; he has destined him to be his heir, and one who will repair the wrongs he has done to Rome. Asked how he regards Caesar, Brutus confesses to a mixture of feelings, anger and horror if he continues to be a tyrant, but an unbounded love if he consents to be a man and a citizen. Then comes the revelation that he is Caesar's son. This only adds to the force of Brutus's appeals. He begs Caesar to prove himself the father of the Roman people; only then will he be able to claim Brutus as his son. Caesar is moved, but refuses to be influenced by emotion and claims that things have gone too far for any retreat to be possible. The interview ends with Caesar still believing that Brutus cannot turn against his father and Brutus still hoping that Caesar can become a true father.

Firm and determined though he appeared to be with Caesar, Brutus is not unmoved by what he has heard. But strengthened by Porcia, who reminds him that he is her husband and bears the name of Brutus, and by Cassius, who argues that a citizen of Rome has no father, he resolves not to be deflected by nature from his duty to his country. He still believes that Caesar will restore Rome's liberty, and when the Senate meets he announces that he is Caesar's son and proud of it because Caesar is going to step down from his position of dictator. He is soon disillusioned. Caesar has resolved to take Brutus with him on his expedition against the Parthians, leaving Antony in charge of Rome; he is no tyrant, but he expects to be obeyed. In that case, says Brutus, let us obey him as true citizens should, by killing him. The play ends with Brutus addressing the people. He informs them that the tyrant whom he has killed was his father. He mourns for Caesar, and though he deserves to die for killing him, he must live for the sake of Rome's future. All must mourn for Caesar but none should wish him alive; their task is rather to restore full liberty to Rome.

More than any previous play about the Ides of March *Bruto Secondo* is a political play. It is dedicated (in the fateful year 1789) to the future people of Italy. The dedication showed at once that the play carried a contemporary message and that the Italian people were not yet ready to respond to it. The Romans of the time of Brutus were not so very different. As Brutus says in the course of the play, they might be aroused to virtue, but only for a short time; they were too corrupted to serve as a foundation for a restored freedom. Alfieri was well aware that the death of Caesar did not lead to the restoration of freedom, but he chose to end with its triumph, with a speech from Brutus rather than one from Antony. Brutus's eloquence inspires his listeners to remember if only for a brief moment that they can once more be the Roman people. This Alfieri considered was the point at which to end the tragedy if the aim was to bring out the most noble ideal which it presented, 'a just and unbounded love of liberty'.[10]

Alfieri might well have included the French with the Italians of his own day and the Romans under Caesar among those who were not ready for liberty, for when he visited France, after writing *Bruto Secondo*, and saw what was done in the name of liberty he was appalled. Others too were disillusioned, and to Wordsworth their disillusion recalled those words in which Brutus was said to have addressed virtue before his death.

> But history, Time's slavish scribe, will tell
> How rapidly the zealots of the cause
> Disbanded – or in hostile ranks appear'd;
> Some, tired of honest service! these, outdone,
> Disgusted, therefore, or appall'd, by aims
> Of fiercer zealots – so confusion reign'd,
> And the more faithful were compell'd to exclaim,
> As Brutus did to virtue, 'Liberty,
> I worshipp'd thee, and find thee but a shade.[11]

Hitherto Brutus's words had been either censured or excused as the utterance of one unhappily ignorant of the Christian revelation; now there were those who could accept them as true to nature and to their own experience. Such was the case with Leopardi. To him there was no utterance recorded from antiquity 'more pitiful and terrifying and at the same time, humanly speaking, more true' than Brutus's address to virtue.[12] It inspired his *Bruto Minore*, a poem very different in spirit from Alfieri's play of a generation earlier bearing a similar title. He pictures Brutus after the disaster of

Philippi, alone in the moonlit night, determined on death, indignantly addressing the unfeeling powers who care so little for human beings, and claiming the right of the brave man to take his own life. The soliloquy ends with the words, in G. L. Bickersteth's translation:

> No suppliant I of Heaven's or Hell's deaf lords,
> No aid from thee I crave,
> Vile Earth, nor, dying, call on Night to save;
> Nor thee, that gildest death with one last beam,
> Fame in the after-years. The scoffer's grave
> Could sobs placate, could gifts adorn or words
> Of the base crowd? Fast stride
> The times from bad to worse; we ill confide
> Unto degenerate sons
> Honour to noble mind, the last supreme
> Revenge for all it suffered. Nay, on me
> Let the foul bird flap down to feast at once;
> Torn my unknown corpse be
> By wild beast and wild weather,
> The wind disperse both name and fame together.

It is magnificent but it is not Brutus. Indeed these last lines directly contradict his last words as reported by Plutarch, which show him far from indifferent to his future fame. It is Leopardi who speaks, Leopardi the sickly, unhappy scholar-poet, who had himself contemplated suicide, and who uses Brutus as the mouthpiece for his own feelings at once despairing and defiant.

Since the eighteenth century Roman themes have not been much in favour with dramatists. The present century has, however, seen at least one new play on the death of Caesar, Enrico Corradini's *Giulio Cesare*, first written in 1902 but revised in 1926. Corradini was an Italian nationalist writer, a precursor of Fascism, who welcomed Mussolini's assumption of power. He regarded Julius Caesar as 'the greatest Hero of the heroic people of Rome', and expressed the hope, to quote from the English translation of the preface to his play, that he, 'an Italian of this victorious epoch', would be able 'to cast upon the new fertility of Italy at least the seed of the drama of the Race, the supreme form of art, the sacred representation, the rite both mystic and heroic'.[13] This turgid bombast leads us to expect the worst, and the play, though it was thought worthy of translation into English, is indeed poor stuff.

It is a good deal more favourable to Brutus than might have been expected. The author appears to regard him as representing one side of the true Roman tradition. In a pronouncement of oracular obscurity he tells Caesar that 'Rome is freedom', that she is 'the new humanity itself that we carry in us . . . severe and proud in conformity with the nature of the people'; and Caesar acknowledges that Brutus raises him to 'lofty Roman thoughts'. There seems to be some influence of Alfieri when Brutus stands up to Caesar and appeals to him to restore Rome's freedom, and again when Caesar addresses him as son. The relationship is, however, sentimentalized as it was not in Alfieri, or in Voltaire before him. 'This is the way,' says Caesar at one point, 'I used to take your face in my hands when you were a child. O fruit of my greatest love, I see your features.'

It is through novels, however, more than in drama that the twentieth century has attempted to reconstruct the Roman world. Jack Lindsay, Phyllis Bentley, Thornton Wilder, Rex Warner, and probably others, have published novels dealing with the last years of the Republic and in particular with the life and personality of Caesar.[14] Of these the only one that need concern us is Phyllis Bentley's *Freedom Farewell*, a vivid and readable book which ends with Brutus's suicide at Philippi. The author recreates the characters in her story with all the professional skill of a best-selling novelist, among them Brutus, who is depicted as sensitive, ingenuous, idealistic, horrified when he learns what his agents have done in Cyprus. The book was published in 1936, when its title was very relevant to the contemporary European situation, and its publisher was Gollancz, of the Left Book Club. We expect then some political message, and we find it in the last thoughts of Brutus before he puts an end to his life. He asks himself how it is that the Romans have let freedom slip away, and answers by blaming the arrogance and folly of the patricians, the selfishness of the wealthy, timidity, confusion and delay on the part of the moderates, greed and stupidity on the part of the people. He refers to the weaknesses of Rome's military arrangements, her system of justice and her provincial rule. 'Perhaps too,' he adds, 'we depend too much on our slaves to make life pleasant for us; perhaps no man can be truly free who is surrounded by slaves.' As for the Ides of March, he now regrets it. 'The Republic was too small for Caesar; in trying to make it great he broke it. So we were fools to hope to end despotism by murder; we forgot that a man always leaves inheritors, who share what he leaves between them . . . It was wrong to let Caesar become a despot, and wrong to murder; we should have defended ourselves strongly from the first, within the Republic's law. Law brings forth law, but the sword only the sword. Once override the law, and the law is robbed of its force, its power of protection.' These are admirable sentiments, but they do not sound much like the thoughts of the historical Brutus. He would not have been so conscious of the weaknesses of the society in which he lived; it is safe to say that he would have had no doubts about slavery; and all the evidence we have suggests that he felt no regret for his action in killing Caesar.

Finally a post-war Brutus, that of Roy Fuller in his poem *The Ides of March*.[15] Brutus is in his orchard soliloquizing before the conspirators come to join him. The scene recalls *Julius Caesar*, but in Shakespeare Brutus's thoughts are on Caesar and the grounds for putting him to death; Fuller makes him more interested in himself than in his cause. He analyses his feelings in a cool ironic spirit.

> And now I am about
> To cease being a fellow traveller, about
> To select from several complex panaceas,
> Like a shy man confronted with a box
> Of chocolates, the plainest after all.
> I am aware that in my conscious wish
> To rid the empire of a tyrant there
> Is something that will give me personal pleasure;
> That usually one's father's death occurs
> About the time one becomes oneself a father.
> These subtleties are not, I think, important –
> No more than that I shall become a traitor,
> Technically, to my class, my friend, my country.
> No, the important thing is to remove
> Guilt from this orchard, which is why I have
> Invited here those men of action with
> Their simpler motives and their naked knives.

The dawn comes and he sees the silhouettes of some muffled figures.

> It is embarrassing to find oneself
> Involved in this clumsy masquerade. There still
> Is time to send a servant with a message:
> 'Brutus is not at home'; time to postpone
> Relief and fear. Yet plucking nervously
> The pregnant twigs, I stay. Good morning comrades.

We think by way of contrast not only of the scene in Brutus's orchard in Shakespeare but also of the soliloquy which Leopardi put into his mouth on a different occasion. There is a striking difference between the impassioned rhetoric of Leopardi's Brutus and the dry detached tone of Fuller's. Each belongs to its author and his age and country; neither belongs to the historical Brutus. Fuller's Brutus is hardly the man to whom the other conspirators looked up as their leader, the man of whom Caesar said 'quicquid vult valde vult'.

As this survey has shown, when imaginative writers – poets, dramatists, novelists – reconstruct the past there is always something of themselves in their reconstructions. They should be able to teach us something about the past. They have gifts which the learned often lack; they can see into the human heart, they can bring the past to life. Yet, reluctantly perhaps, we must go back from them to the ancient sources. We must ask ourselves whether the Brutus of Shakespeare, Voltaire, Alfieri, Leopardi and others is really the historical Brutus, the man whom we know, as far as we can know him, from Plutarch, from Cicero, and from his own letters. But if the answer must often be in the negative at least we will have learnt something; we will have been reminded that Brutus was a human being.

NOTES

For classical texts the abbreviations used are those of Liddell and Scott's Greek-English Lexicon and the Oxford Latin Dictionary.

Notes to I 1

1 M. H. Crawford, *Roman Republican Coinage* (Cambridge 1974) No. 433 1 & 2 (p. 455). For the date see p. 88.

2 Cic. *Phil.* 2.26, *Att.* 13.40.1; Nep. *Att.* 18.3

3 Cic. *Brut.* 229, 324; Vell. 2.72

4 See Douglas on Cic. *Brut.* 324. Douglas adopts Nipperdey's emendation of *decem* to *sedecim*, which brings Cicero into line with Velleius. To the evidence given by Douglas in favour of the later date one might add that Nepos (*Att.* 8.1–2) uses the word *adulescens* of Brutus after the assassination of Caesar. Brutus's quaestorship rests on the rather uncertain testimony of *Vir. ill.* 82.3–4.

5 Plut. *Brut.* 5.2–4; Suet. *Jul.* 50.2

6 Plut. *Brut.* 5.2; Suet. *Jul.* 82.3

7 Plut. *Brut.* 5.3; Suet. *Jul.* 50.2; Cic. *Att.* 2.24.3

8 Suet. *Jul.* 82.2; cf Dio 44.19.5

9 Suet. *Gram.* 13

10 Plut. *Brut.* 2.5

11 Cic. *Brut.* 332, *Orat.* 105; Plut. *Brut.* 2.4, 52.6–8. For Brutus's study in Rhodes see *Vir. ill.* 82.1; for Empylus as a Rhodian Quint. *Inst.* 10.6.4

12 Plut. *Brut.* 2.3–3

13 M. Radin, *Marcus Brutus* (Oxford 1939) 233

14 Cic. *Ac.* 2.132

15 Cic. *Fin.* 5.81, *Tusc.* 5.22

16 In *Paradoxa* proem. Cicero classes himself and Brutus together, distinguishing them from the Stoic Cato.

17 Cic. *Att.* 15.9.1, 13.40.1

18 Cic. *Orat.* 110; Plin. *Nat.* 34.82; Mart. 2.77.4, 14.171

19 Cic. *Att.* 13.8 (Caelius Antipater), 12.5b (Fannius); Plut. *Brut.* 4.8 (Polybius)

20 Tac. *Dial.* 21.6; cf. Plin. *Ep.* 5.3.5

21 *Vir. ill.* 82.2

22 Cic. *Att.* 10.10.5, *Fam.* 9.26.2

23 Cic. *Att.* 2.24.2–3

24 Suet. *Jul.* 21; Plut. *Caes.* 14.3, *Pomp.* 47.4; App. *B.C.* 2.14

25 Münzer in *R.E.* II 4 1776; cf. Syme, *Roman Revolution* (Oxford 1939) 34

26 Cic. *Att.* 4.18.2–3, *Q.fr.* 3.4.1, 3.5 & 6.4, 3.8.4; Crawford, *Roman Republican Coinage* 455–6

27 Cic. *Fam.* 3.10.9, 3.13.2

28 Cic. *Brut.* 22, 192, 324. In addition to his defence of Appius Claudius Brutus wrote a *laudatio* of his father-in-law, presumably on his death in 48. Keil, *G.L.* I.367 (Diomedes)

29 Quint. *Inst.* 3.6.93

30 Quint. *Inst.* 9.3.95; Sen. *Con.* 10.1.8; Malcovati, *O.R.F.* I.463. The speech, according to Quintilian, was *De Dictatura Pompei*. A dictatorship was considered but rejected in favour of appointment as sole consul. For another attack on Pompey, by Helvius Mancia, mentioning the elder Brutus among his victims, see V. Max. 6.2.8

31 Cic. *Fam.* 3.11.3

32 Cic. *Att.* 6.1.3; cf. *Fam.* 15.14.6

33 Cic. *Att.* 5.21.10–13, 6.1.3–8, 6.2.7–9
34 Cic. *Att.* 6.1.6–7 (Shackleton Bailey's translation)
35 Cic. *Att.* 6.2.10
36 D. R. Shackleton Bailey, *Cicero's Letters to Atticus* (Cambridge 1965–70) I.29n. Cf. Syme, *Roman Revolution* 57 n.4
37 Plut. *Brut.* 4.5, 5.1

38 Luc. 2.234–325
39 Cic. *Att.* 11.4a
40 Plut. *Brut.* 6.3–4
41 Caes. *Civ.* 3.106
42 Cic. *Att.* 14.1.2
43 Cic. *Brut.* 156, 250
44 Plut. *Brut.* 6.11, *Comp. Dion. Brut.* 5
45 Cic. *Fam.* 15.15

Notes to I 2

1 Cic. *Brut.* 11–12, 330. Hendrikson in *A.J.P.* lx (1939) 401–13 argues that the 'letter' was Brutus's *De Virtute*, dedicated to Cicero, and his conclusions are accepted by Douglas (edition of *Brutus*, xi). This is unlikely. Elsewhere Cicero uses the word *liber* for *De Virtute* (*Fin.* 1.8, *Tusc.* 5.1) and he would hardly have called it an *epistula*. Moreover, Brutus's letter was sent from Asia and his *De Virtute* is unlikely to have been completed before he left for Italy. It referred to his visit to Marcellus at Mitylene, which was probably made in the course of his return journey.
2 Quint. *Inst.* 10.1.123; Tac. *Dial.* 21.5. More favourable references in Quint. *Inst.* 12.10.11 and Tac. *Dial.* 25.3–4
3 Cic. *Brut.* 22
4 Cic. *Brut.* 331–2
5 Boissier, *Cicero and his Friends* (E.T. 6th ed. n.d.) 332–3; *Historia* 7 (1958) 91; cf. *Cicero* (ed. T. A. Dorey, 1965) 198. For criticism of Balsdon see H. Bengtson, *SB Bayerische Akademie der Wissenschaften* 1970, 14–15.

6 Cic. *Fam.* 4.4.3; *Pro Marcello* passim
7 Cic. *Brut.* 23
8 Cic. *Orat.* 40; Quint. *Inst.* 9.4.63, 76
9 Tac. *Dial.* 18.4–5; Quint. *Inst.* 12.1.22, 12.10.12
10 Cic. *Orat.* 1–2, 34–5, 52, 140, 147, 174, 238, *Att.* 14.20.3
11 Plut. *Brut.* 2.5; J. A. K. Thomson, *The Classical Background of English Literature* (1948) 185; *Julius Caesar*, ed. J. Dover Wilson (Cambridge 1949) xix
12 See A. E. Douglas, edition of *Brutus*, xii–xiv. I wrongly counted Brutus as an Atticist in my *Rhetoric at Rome* (1953) 80
13 Cic. *Brut.* 284; *Orat.* 23, 28; *Tusc.* 2.3
14 Cic. *Orat.* 33–4
15 Ibid. 35
16 Cic. *Fam.* 6.7.4
17 Plut. *Brut.* 40.7
18 Cic. *Rep.* 6.15; *Tusc.* 1.74; *Off.* 1.112
19 Cic. *Att.* 12.21.1
20 Ibid. 13.46.2
21 Ibid. 12.13.1, 12.14.4
22 Cic. *ad Brut.* 1.9.1–2

23 Cic. *Att.* 12.14.4
24 Ibid. 13.9.2, 13.10.3
25 Cic. *Att.* 12.32.2; *ad Brut.* 1.7.1, 1.14.1; App. *B.C.* 4.104. In *ad Brut.* 1.7.2 Brutus writes to Cicero 'Bibulum noli dimittere e sinu tuo', which suggests that Bibulus was then in Italy. If so, either he had returned from Athens or he never went there (In *Att.* 12.32.2 Cicero had merely heard that he intended to go). Plut. *Brut.* 23.6 suggests that he was with Brutus on the latter's departure from Italy, and one might deduce from App. *B.C.* 4.38 that he went to join his step-father in order to avoid the proscriptions.
26 Plut. *Brut.* 13.3 exaggerates her youth and that of her son.
27 Plut. *Brut.* 13.4
28 Cic. *Att.* 13.22.4
29 M. Radin, *Marcus Brutus* 40

30 Cic. *Att.* 12.36.2, 13.11.1
31 Cic. *Att.* 13.23.1
32 Cic. *Att.* 13.35–6.3
33 The *Paradoxa*, written before the *Brutus*, was also dedicated to him.
34 Cic. *Tusc.* 1.1, 5.121
35 Sen. *Cons. Helv.* 8.1, 9.4–7; Quint. *Inst.* 10.1.123. After the murder of Marcellus at Piraeus on his way home from exile Brutus in a letter to Cicero exonerated Caesar from complicity (*Att.* 13.10.3). Some modern writers regard this as of some political significance.
36 M. Brutus in eo libro quem περὶ καθήκοντος inscripsit. Sen. *Ep.* 95.45. Priscian quotes from 'De Officiis'. VI 6 (Keil *G.L.* II 199)
37 Sen. *Ep.* 95.45
38 Cic. *Tusc.* 5.1
39 Cic. *Tusc.* 5.4–5

Notes to I 3

1 Cic. *Att.* 13.40.1; 13.39.2; 13.44.1
2 Plut. *Brut.* 7.1–5
3 Cic. *Fam.* 6.6.10; 15.15.3
4 Cic. *Fam.* 15.16, 15.18
5 Cic. *Fam.* 15.16.3; 15.19.2–3
6 Lucr. 5.1127
7 Cic. *Fam.* 15.19.4
8 Plut. *Brut.* 9.1–4; Cic. *Phil.* 2.26
9 Plut. *Caes.* 57.1
10 Suet. *Jul.* 76
11 Cic. *Mil.* 80
12 Cic. *Rep.* 1.50, 65, 68; 2.47–49
13 Cic. *Att.* 14.1.2; cf. Plut. *Brut.* 6.7
14 Plut. *Caes.* 62.5; *Ant.* 11.3
15 Dio 44.12–14. Gelzer (*R.E.* X

1 989–990) thinks Dio's version more likely to be right. Nicolaus of Damascus (*F.G.H.* II A (1921) 402) simply says that the leading conspirators were Decimus Brutus, Cassius and Marcus Brutus.
16 Plut. *Brut.* 10.1–2
17 Suet. *Jul.* 80.3; Plut. *Brut.* 9.5–7; *Caes.* 62.4
18 Plut. *Brut.* 13.3–11
19 Cic. *Div.* 2.110; Suet. *Jul.* 79.2–80.1; Dio 44.15.4
20 Cic. *Att.* 15.11.2
21 Nic. Dam. *F.G.H.* II A, 409; Dio 44.20–21
22 App. *B.C.* 2.17.121–2. Plut. *Brut.* 18.7–13 has Brutus make a

public speech on the Capitol before coming down and making
another in the forum.
23 Cic. *Att.* 15.1a.2
24 App. *B.C.* 2.137–141
25 Cic. *Phil.* 2.30; *Att.* 14.10.1
26 Cic. *Fam.* 11.1.2–3
27 Cic. *Phil.* 2.31
28 Cic. *Phil.* 10.7
29 Cic. *Att.* 14.10.1
30 Cic. *Att.* 15.4.2; 15.20.2
31 Nep. *Att.* 8.2–4; Cic. *Att.*
14.20.3–4; 15.4.2
32 Cic. *Att.* 14.9.2 (similar sentiments elsewhere)
33 Cic. *Att.* 14.15.1; 14.16.2;
14.17a; 14.19.1
34 Cic. *Att.* 14.18.4; 15.5.1
35 Cic. *Fam.* 11.2
36 Cic. *Att.* 15.9.1; 15.10
37 Cic. *Att.* 15.11.1–3
38 Cic. *Att.* 16.4.1, 4; 16.5.3;
16.7.5
39 Cic. *Att.* 15.26.1
40 Cic. *Att.* 16.2.3; 16.4.1; 16.5.1;
Phil. 1.36; 2.31; 10.8. In *Att.* 16.5.1

Cicero reports that he has given
Brutus news about Accius's *Tereus*
and adds 'ille Brutum putabat'.
Shackleton Bailey writes of Brutus's mistake, and Gelzer (*R.E.* X
1 997–8) assumed that C. Antonius, Mark Antony's brother, who
as praetor acted for Brutus in
connection with the games, had
the *Tereus* substituted for the
Brutus. Could Cicero's remark be
simply a joke?
41 Cic. *Phil.* 1.8; Vell. 2.62.3
42 Cic. *Att.* 16.7.7
43 Cic. *Fam.* 12.25.3
44 According to Cic. *Phil.* 10.8
Cassius's fleet followed Brutus a
few days later. But two letters
from Cicero to Cassius belonging
to the end of September and beginning of October give no indication that he had then left Italy.
(*Fam.* 12.2 and 3)
45 Cic. *Att.* 16.7.1
46 Plut. *Brut.* 23.2–6
47 Cic. *Phil.* 1.9

Notes to I 4

1 Appian's statement that Caesar
had promised Cassius Syria and
Brutus Macedonia (*B.C.* 3.2) is
commonly rejected by modern
scholars.
2 Cic. *Att.* 14.12.2
3 Cic. *Fam.* 12.3
4 Plut. *Brut.* 24.1; Dio 47.20. See
A. E. Raubitschek in *Phoenix* XI
(1957) 5.
5 Cic. *Off.* 3.5–6
6 Plut. *Brut.* 24.2
7 Cic. *Phil.* 10.9; cf. 10.14
8 Cic. *Fam.* 10.28.2. In November

44 Cicero was writing his *De
Officiis* for the benefit of his son on
the assumption that he was studying philosophy; in the course of it
he refers to his son's military
exploits at Pharsalus as something
that would not recur. *Off.* 2.45
9 Cic. *Att.* 15.13.4
10 Plut. *Brut.* 24.4–25.2; App.
B.C. 3.63
11 Cic. *Phil.* 10.24, *Fam.* 12.5.1
12 Cic. *Phil.* 10.25–6
13 Cic. *Phil.* 10.18–19
14 Cic. *Phil.* 11.27–8

15 Cic. *Phil.* 4.13
16 Cic. *ad Brut.* 2.3.2; 2.4.3; 2.5.3–5
17 Cic. *ad Brut.* 1.2a.2; 1.3.3
18 Cic. *ad Brut.* 1.3a; 1.4.2
19 *The Correspondence of Cicero*, ed. Tyrrell and Purser VI (Dublin 1899) xliv; Heitland, *The Roman Republic* (Cambridge 1909) III 405
20 Plut. *Brut.* 26.6 to 28.1
21 Cic. *ad Brut.* 1.13; 1.12; 1.15.11–13; 1.18.6
22 Cic. *ad Brut.* 1.17
23 Cic. *ad Brut.* 1.16. Watt dates this letter doubtfully to July. Bengtson (*SB. Bayerische Akademie der Wissenschaften* 1970, 16 and 32) dates it to May. Tyrrell and Purser changed from May in their first edition to July in the second. Raubitschek (*Phoenix* XI 1957, 6) dates it to before December 44. Stockton (*Cicero, A Political Biography*, Oxford 1971, 326) suggests December 44 or January 43. In favour of a late date is the fact that Cicero's references to Octavian in letters written in April do not give the impression that

Brutus had already expressed such severe criticisms. The evidence of Plutarch (*Brut.* 22.4–6) is confusing. He quotes some criticisms of Cicero's attitude to Octavian which he attributes to Brutus's 'first letters'. His summary is nearer to 1.17, the letter to Atticus, than to 1.16, but the statement which he attributes to Brutus that he has not definitely decided on either war or peace is in neither letter. He quotes one sentence, 'Our ancestors could not endure even gentle despots', which is near to but not identical with *dominum ne parentem quidem maiores nostri voluerunt esse* in the letter to Atticus (1.17.6).
24 Cic. *ad Brut.* 1.15.5–6
25 Cic. *ad Brut.* 1.9
26 Plut. *Brut.* 53.6–7
27 Plut. *Brut.* 53.5; Val. Max. 4.6.5; Mart. 1.42; App. *B.C.* 4.136; Dio 47.49.
28 Cic. *ad Brut.* 1.10.4; 1.14.2; 1.15.12; 1.18.1–2
29 Plut. *Brut.* 28.1–2

Notes to I 5

1 Cic. *Fam.* 12.11
2 Cic. *Phil.* 10.26; *ad Brut.* 1.5.1
3 Cic. *ad Brut.* 1.2.1–2
4 Brutus *Ep. Graec.* 1 (quoted Plut. *Brut.* 2.6) The authenticity of Brutus's Greek letters has been disputed. Those which I have used are accepted as genuine by L. Torraca in his edition, Naples 1959.
5 Brutus *Ep. Graec.* 61, 63
6 M. Brutus adversus Thracas

parum prospere rem gessit. Livy *Epit.* 122
7 Hor. *Sat.* 1.7
8 App. *B.C.* 4.71–81
9 Brutus *Ep. Graec.* 25 (quoted Plut. *Brut.* 2.8), 27
10 Plut. *Brut.* 30–32
11 Plut. *Brut.* 36–7
12 Val. Max. 1.8.8
13 Plut. *Brut.* 29.9
14 M. H. Crawford, *Roman Re-*

publican Coinage 508; Dio 47.25.
For Lorenzino de' Medici see
p. **90**; for Brutus rings in the
eighteenth century see p. **99**.
15 Crawford, *Roman Republican
Coinage* 514–18; Plut. *Brut.* 24.7.
Crawford's contention (p. 741)
that Apollo suggested liberty is
based on very tenuous grounds.
16 So Appian, *B.C.* 4.108, followed by most modern historians.
Plutarch (*Brut.* 38.5) says the Republicans were inferior in numbers, Dio (47.38.2) that they were
superior.
17 See Front. *Strat.* 4.2.1
18 Plut. *Brut.* 38.5–7, 39.1–2
19 Plut. *Brut.* 40.5–9
20 App. *B.C.* 4.109
21 It is said that Octavian's doctor
was warned in a dream. According
to the flattering version of Velleius
(2.70) and Valerius Maximus
(1.7.1) Octavian was brought out
of camp into line of battle in spite
of his illness.
22 App. *B.C.* 4.113. The first
version is that of Plutarch (*Brut.*
43) and Velleius (2.70)
23 Plut. *Brut.* 46.1–2. Cf. App.
B.C. 4.118
24 App. *B.C.* 4.122–5
25 Plut. *Brut.* 51–2. For a rather
different version of Brutus's end
see App. *B.C.* 4.131
26 Dio 47.49.1–2 (*Trag. Adesp.*
374 N.) The only confirmation of
Dio's story is in Florus *Epit.*
2.17.11, where after mentioning
the capture of Octavian's camp by
one side and Cassius's by the other
in the first battle of Philippi he
adds the comment: 'sed quanto
efficacior est fortuna quam virtus!

et quam verum est quod moriens
efflavit, non in re sed in verbo esse
virtutem! victoriam illi proelio
error dedit'. Editors either insert
the name Brutus before *efflavit* or
assume that he is the subject,
though he has not been mentioned
in the previous sentence and his
suicide is yet to come. Would they
do so if they did not know Dio?
Could it not be that Hercules is the
subject of *efflavit* rather than Brutus?
27 Victorius, *Variae Lectiones*
(1553) xxiii 2; J.-B. Crevier in
Rollin's *Ancient History* (E.T. 1768)
X 45; cf. Bayle, *Dictionnaire Historique et Critique* (ed. 1730) s.v.
Brutus, Marc Junius; Diderot and
d'Alembert, *Encyclopédie* (1751–
77) s.v. Athéisme; Rousseau,
Oeuvres Complètes (Paris 1959–69)
IV 589 (the Savoyard Vicar in
Emile). Among modern historians
who accept Dio's story are Gelzer
(*R.E.* X i 1017), Charlesworth
(*C.A.H.* X 25) and Syme (*Roman
Revolution* 206). One of the few
sceptics in the past was Adam
Ferguson, *History of the Progress
and Termination of the Roman Republic*, 1805 ed. V 362.
28 Plut. *Brut.* 53.4; *Comp. Dion.
Brut.* 5.1; App. *B.C.* 4.135; Suet.
Aug. 13; Dio 47.49.2
29 Boissier, *Cicero and his Friends*
(E.T. n.d.) 309 n.
30 V. Gardthausen, *Augustus und
seine Zeit* (Leipzig 1891) 17–18;
J. M. C. Toynbee, *Roman Historical Portraits* (1978) 62–3
31 Boissier, *Cicero and his Friends*
309
32 Cic. *Att.* 14.20.5

33 Cic. *Att.* 14.17a.5 (Shackleton Bailey's translation)
34 Plut. *Brut.* 29.3
35 Cic. *Att.* 14.14.2; *ad Brut.* 2.5.6
36 J. H. Newman, 'Liberal Knowledge in Relation to Religion' in *Lectures on the Nature and Scope of University Education.*
37 Dio 47.21. Ronald Syme (*Tacitus*, Oxford 1958, 530) makes Brutus an anti-imperialist on the

strength of what is surely a misinterpretation of the sentence from his speech *de dictatura Pompei* (see p. **17**)
38 *Mon. Anc.* 1
39 Plut. *Brut.* 47.3–7. According to Appian (*B.C.* 4.123) Brutus did know of the naval success before the second battle.
40 Tac. *Hist.* 1.1
41 Plut. *Brut.* 53.3
42 Hor. *Carm.* 2.7.11

Notes to II 1

1 Cic. *Phil.* 2.114; *Att.* 14.11.1; Cf. *Phil.* 10.7; *Att.* 14.4.2, 14.6.1, 14.14.3
2 Cic. *Off.* 3.19, 32. Cf. 1.26; 2.23, 27, 84; 3.84
3 Cic. *Fam.* 11.28.2–4
4 Ov. *Pont.* 1.1.24. Plutarch mentions memoirs of Brutus by his stepson Bibulus, by Volumnius and by Empylus.
5 Tac. *Ann.* 4.34
6 Plut. *Comp. Dion. et Brut.* 5. But the rhetorician Albucius nearly got into trouble while pleading a case at Milan when he invoked Brutus as a champion of liberty. Suet. *Rhet.* 6
7 Tac. *Ann.* 3.76, 4.34–5. See Sen. *Ben.* 3.26–7 for the difference in atmosphere between the reigns of Augustus and Tiberius.
8 Tac. *Ann.* 16.22.9
9 Juv. 5.36–7; Plin. *Ep.* 1.17.3; Fergus Millar, *The Emperor in the Roman World* (1977) 89–90
10 Val. Max. 1.27, 3.2.15, 6.4.5; Plut. *Comp. Dion et Brut.* 2.2
11 Sen. *Ben.* 2.20, *Cons. Helv.* 9

12 Sen. *Ben.* 2.20
13 Plut. *Comp. Dion. et Brut.* 3.4–8
14 Suet. *Vita Lucani*
15 Luc. 9.17–18
16 Luc. 2.281–4
17 Luc. 7.588–96
18 Luc. 10.341–4
19 Vell. 2.72.2
20 See esp. Plut. *Brut.* 29.3–8
21 Juv. 14.41–3
22 M. Aurel. Ant. 1.14
23 Dante, *Inferno* xxxiv 61–7
24 Dante, *De Monarchia* II ch. 5
25 Virgil, *Aen.* 8.670
26 Chaucer, *Monk's Tale* 3896
27 Thomas Elyott, *Governour* III vi; John Carion, *Chronicles* (E.T. 1550) lxxxv; *An auncient Historie and exquisite Chronicle of the Romanes warres both Civile and Foren* (1578) Dedication.
28 John of Salisbury, *Policraticus* III xv, IV i, VII xxv, VIII vii, xvii, xix.
29 Aquinas, *Scriptum super libros Sententiarum* II dist. 449 II a 2
30 Aquinas, *De Regimine Principis*

III (21–25), VI (44–51). Aquinas's *De Regno* was combined with a work by another writer *De Regimine Principis* and the latter title was given to the combined work, which is included in the works of Aquinas.

31 It was not only Protestants who quoted the precedent of Eglon. See Aquinas *De Regimine Principis* VI (45)

32 Mariana, *De Rege et Regis Institutione* (1599) Bk. 1 ch. 5

33 *A Defence of Liberty against Tyrants* (reprint of 1689 translation of *Vindiciae contra Tyrannos*, 1924) 122, 192–4

34 Petrarch, *Epistolae* (ed. Fracassetti, Florence 1859) III 426 (*Variae* 48); Bocaccio, *De Casibus Virorum Illustrium* II

35 See *Coluccio Salutati's Traktat*

'*Vom Tyrannen*' edited by A. von Martin, Berlin and Leipzig, 1913.

36 H. Baron, *The Crisis of the early Italian Renaissance* (Princeton, New Jersey, 1966) 156, referring to Salutati's *De Fato et Fortuna* (1399)

37 Leonardo Bruni, *Dialogi ad Petrum Histrum* (ed. G. Kirner, Leghorn 1889) 52–3, translation by H. Baron, *The Crisis of the early Italian Renaissance* 49–50

38 Cristoforo Landino, in *Opere di Dante* (1512) 191

39 See D. J. Gordon, 'Giannotti, Michelangelo and the Cult of Brutus' in *Fritz Saxl 1890–1945* (1957) 281–296

40 *De' Giorni che Dante consumò nel cercare l'Inferno e'l Purgatorio, Dialogi di Donato Giannotti* (Florence 1859) 54–63

Notes to II 2

1 Hobbes, *Leviathan* Part 2, chs. 29 and 21

2 *Works of John Milton* (New York) 5 (1932) 19; 7 (1932) 324–6, 336; 18 (1938) 163

3 James Thomson, *Seasons*, Summer 1527–31. Cf. Memoir in Algernon Sidney, *Discourses concerning Government* (1763) 37

4 Sidney, *Discourses* I 3, II 15; A. C. Ewald, *Life and Times of the Hon. Algernon Sydney* (1873) I 198, 309

5 Matthew Tindal, *The Judgment of Dr Prideaux in condemning the Murder of Julius Caesar maintained* (1721) 41–2; A. H. Nethercot, *Abraham Cowley, The Muse's Han-*

nibal (Oxford, 1931) 153, 199

6 James Dyer, *The Ruins of Rome*, 1740 (Addison had similarly adapted Virgil in his *Letter from Italy*, 1701); Lord Lyttelton, *An Epistle to Mr Pope* 1730; George Keate, *Ancient and modern Rome*, 1755

7 James Thomson, *Liberty*, Part III 480–83

8 Swift, *Political Tracts 1711–1713*, ed. Herbert Davis (1951) 133–4

9 Digby Cotes, verses prefixed to editions of Addison's *Cato*.

10 Thomson, *Seasons*, Winter 523–6

11 Swift, *Political Tracts 1711–1713* 194, *Gulliver's Travels, Voyage to Laputa* ch. VII

12 Swift, *Irish Tracts 1728–1733*, ed. Herbert Davis (1955) 278; W. B. Stanford, *Ireland and the Classical Tradition* (Dublin 1976) 206, 208–9
13 *Cato's Letters*, Nos. 23, 55, 56 (1720–21)
14 *Cato's Letters* (3rd ed., 1733) xxvi–xxviii
15 Dodsley's *Collection of Poems*, vol. 2 (1775) 212
16 Johnson, *Lives of the Poets*, Akenside; *Edinburgh Review* 92 (1850) 90
17 *The Diary of Sylas Neville 1767–1788* (ed. B. Cozens-Hardy, Oxford 1950) 48, 70 (I owe these references to Mr C. C. Oman); Horace Walpole, *Correspondence* (ed. W. S. Lewis) vol. 29 (1955) 321, 332, 348
18 Bayle, *Dictionnaire Historique et Critique* (ed. 1730) s.v. Brutus, Marc Junius
19 C. Rollin, *The Ancient History* (E.T. 1769) IX 341–2
20 Montesquieu, *Grandeur and Declension of the Romans* (E.T. 1752) 174
21 *Memoir of the Life of Josiah Quincy by his son Josiah Quincy* (Boston, 1825) 468–9; B. Bailyn, *The Ideological Origins of the American Revolution* (Cambridge, Mass. 1971) 23–6; Charles F. Mullet, 'Classical Influences on the American Revolution', *Classical Journal* 35 (1939–40) 92–104; R. C. Simmons, *The American Colonies* (1976) 309
22 Harold T. Parker, *The Cult of Antiquity and the French Revolutionaries* (Chicago 1937) 139–43

Notes to II 3

1 N. Hooke, *Roman History* IV (1771) 251–2, 373
2 Colley Cibber, *Character and Conduct of Cicero* (1747) 229–30
3 Conyers Middleton, *Life of Cicero* (ed. 1810) III 282–3, 302
4 Gibbon, *Memorials of my Life* (ed. G. A. Bonnard, 1966) 75
5 Gibbon, *English Essays* (ed. Patricia B. Craddock, Oxford 1972) 96–106
6 W. Drumann, *Geschichte Roms* (Königsberg, 1834–44) I viii
7 Drumann, *Geschichte Roms* IV 35–43
8 W. Ihne, *Römische Geschichte* VIII (Leipzig 1890) 117; V. Gardthausen, *Augustus und seine Zeit* 18–20. For other German criticisms of Brutus see *R.E.* X i 1019–20
9 T. Arnold, *History of the later Roman Commonwealth* (1845) II 110–11
10 C. Merivale, *History of the Romans under the Empire* (1850–62) III 475–6, repeated with variations in Merivale's *Fall of the Roman Republic* (1853) 444.
11 G. Long, *Decline of the Roman Republic* (1864–74) V 437–9, 465
12 J. A. Froude, *Caesar, A Sketch* (1879) 455–6; W. Warde Fowler, *Julius Caesar and the Foundation of the Roman Imperial System* (1892) 374–7

13 Tyrrell and Purser, *Correspondence of Cicero* V (1897) xxxi, VI (1899) c, cvi, cix, cx. In the second edition of vol. VI Purser, who appears to have been solely responsible for these essays, felt it necessary to answer the question how it was that Brutus had such a reputation with his contemporaries. This he did rather lamely by quoting Bagehot on Francis Horner; like Horner Brutus had 'an atmosphere, a kind of halo'. (cxxii n.)

14 W. E. Heitland, *The Roman Republic* (1909) III 327, 384, 406–7

15 J. V. Duruy, *History of the Roman People* (E.T. 1883–6) III 410 n.

16 Duruy, *History of the Roman People* III 271–2, 379, 399–401, 409–10, 476

17 R. T. Troplong, 'Chute de la République romaine' in *Revue Contemporaine* (1855) vol. 21, 193–243; vol. 23, 385–440

18 H. Taine, *Essais de critique et d'histoire* (1858) 366

19 Michelet, *History of the Roman Republic* (E.T. 1847) 381–2

20 *R.E.* X i 1018

21 *C.A.H.* IX (1934) 735, X (1935) 25

22 Gérard Walter, *Brutus et la fin de la République* (1938); Max Radin, *Marcus Brutus* (1939)

23 Radin, *Marcus Brutus* vii, 228–235. Radin suggests that the Epicurean Atticus would have made a better guide for Brutus than the Stoic Cato. In fact Brutus was in close touch with Atticus; indeed there is more contemporary evidence for Atticus's influence on him than for Cato's.

24 R. Syme, *The Roman Revolution* vii, 4, 57–9, 148, 183, 205

25 Radin, *Marcus Brutus* 5

26 Gibbon, *English Essays* 97–8

27 According to Eduard Meyer, Mommsen, the great admirer of Caesar, applied to Roman history the radical liberalism of 1848, and transferred to the Roman aristocracy his dislike of the reactionary Junkers of that period. Meyer, *Caesars Monarchie und das Principat des Pomejus* (Stuttgart/Berlin, 1918) VII 322–3

Notes to III 1

1 See Jacques Grévin, *Théâtre Complet et Poésies Choisis*, ed. L. Pinvert, (Paris 1922).

2 Donato Giannotti, *Lettere Italiane*, ed. F. Diaz (Milan 1974) 26

3 M. Virdung, *Brutus*, Jena 1596, also in *Juvenilia*, Nürnberg 1598. Virdung (1575–1657) was a professor at Nürnberg and had some reputation as a (Latin) poet.

4 The play was reprinted in 1911 as one of the Malone Society reprints and in 1913 (Tudor Facsimile Texts). A Latin play *Caesar Interfectus* by Richard Eedes was acted at Christ Church Oxford in 1581–2. Only the epilogue survives; text in Geoffrey Bullough (ed.) *Narrative and Dramatic Sources of Shakespeare* V (1964) 194–5

5 Is the character of Lucius due to a confused recollection of Martial's reference to 'Brutus's boy' (see p. 14)?
6 Cic. *Att.* 15.1a.2

7 T. S. Dorsch, The Arden Shakespeare, *Julius Caesar* (1955) xxxiv, cf. xliv
8 Hazlitt, *Works* (ed. P. P. Howe, 1930–4) IV 198

Notes to III 2

1 *Herders Briefe* (Berlin-Weimar, 1970) 118; letter of May 23, 1772, referring to his first draft.
2 On these see A. Scenna, *The Treatment of Ancient History and Legend in Bodmer*, New York 1937. I have not seen *Marcus Brutus*.
3 Published 1636; reprinted with introduction by H. L. Cook, New York 1930.
4 Performed 1635–6, published Paris, 1637
5 Published Paris, 1646
6 Marie-Anne Barbier, *La Mort de César* (Paris, 1710) preface
7 Voltaire, *Oeuvres Complètes* (Paris 1877–85) III 305–10
8 Ibid. III 310. Voltaire actually makes Brutus say that he would kill his father for the sake of the republic, which is not quite what he said in the passage which

Voltaire presumably had in mind, Cic. *Ep. Brut.* 1.16.5 (cf. 1.17.25)
9 See the prefaces to the two plays in A. Conti, *Le quattro tragedie*, Florence 1751.
10 Alfieri, *Tragedie* (ed. N. Bruscoli, Bari 1946–7) III 374–5
11 Wordsworth, *Excursion* III 769–77
12 Leopardi, *Opere* (ed. Solmi, Milan-Naples, 1955–66) I 679
13 E. Corradini, *Julius Caesar*, trans. Helen M. Briggs, 1929
14 Jack Lindsay, *Caesar is Dead*, 1934; Phyllis Bentley, *Freedom Farewell*, 1936; Thornton Wilder, *The Ides of March*, 1948; Rex Warner, *The Young Caesar*, 1958, and *Imperial Caesar*, 1960.
15 In Roy Fuller, *Collected Poems 1936–1961*, previously published in *Brutus's Orchard*, 1957

INDEX